THE B

By the same author:

CALVIN AND THE CALVINISTS

THE BEGINNINGS

*Word and Spirit
in Conversion*

PAUL HELM

THE BANNER OF TRUTH TRUST

THE BANNER OF TRUTH TRUST
3 Murrayfield Road, Edinburgh EH12 6EL
PO Box 621, Carlisle, Pennsylvania 17013, USA

★

© Paul Helm 1986
First published 1986
ISBN 0 85151 470 7

★

Typeset in 10½/12pt Linotron Plantin
At The Spartan Press Ltd, Lymington, Hants
Printed and bound in Great Britain by
Hazell Watson & Viney Limited,
Member of the BPCC Group,
Aylesbury, Bucks

Contents

To
The Rev. W. H. Davies, minister of
the gospel at the Baptist Tabernacle,
Blackpool, since 1955.

Introduction

The American psychologist William James once distinguished between those people who had what he called a 'once-born' religious experience, and those who were 'twice-born'. Whatever the value of this distinction as a way of classifying broad types of religious experience, it is a poor guide to true Christianity. There are not two types of Christian, the once-born and the twice-born. All Christians are, by definition, twice-born. But there are many different kinds of consciously-felt experiences of God's grace, perhaps as many different kinds as there are different people who experience that grace. At one extreme there are those whose awareness of becoming a Christian is slow and almost imperceptible. God has brought them gradually to faith in Christ and to full commitment to Him. There are others, like Paul, or Augustine, whose conversion was a sudden crisis, a distinct, datable event. No doubt William James would classify these two differently. But they are both, by definition, twice-born.

The Bible is emphatic upon the need for all to be converted, and the Christian church, when she is faithful to her biblical calling, is insistent, in her preaching and missionary work, upon the gaining of converts.

Why is this? Why is conversion necessary? Why is the call to conversion central in the teaching of the Christian church? These are important questions to think about, and not only for those who are not Christians. For there is the danger of Christians themselves losing sight of the goal, and of thinking that conversions are needed 'in order to keep the church going'. Just as a bureaucracy instead of serving the public can come to shuffle paper in order to keep the jobs of the bureaucrats themselves, so it is possible for the church to lower her horizons, and to think that conversions matter simply because they add to the strength of the church, or because they result in increased power or influence or reputation. Taking this attitude, the church becomes interested in gaining followers for its own sake.

So why is conversion vital, and why is the church being faithful to her mandate when she calls for conversions? The basic answer is because the church, in proclaiming the good news of the gospel, is the human agent in God's plan for the formation of a new humanity under Christ. The church does not exist merely to perpetuate herself as an institution, or to gain social or political influence, but to re-call men and women to the knowledge and service of God. Conversion is a necessary part of the response to this call. The plight of men and women before God is such that they need to be born again, to be converted. The phrase 'born again', though at present debased into a trivial political slogan, describes the basic spiritual need of all people.

Even within evangelical religion, where, in the past, these matters have been understood and emphasised, there is now a lack of definiteness. Terms such as 'regeneration', 'conversion' and 'effectual calling', with precise meanings and clear biblical support, have been eclipsed by 'Take Jesus into your life', 'Know Jesus as your own personal Saviour', 'Give your heart to Jesus'. It cannot be too strongly emphasised that this change is not merely verbal and therefore of no real importance. Such is the close relationship between language, thought and experience that vague and indefinite language is invariably accompanied by vague and indefinite experience.

The Bible speaks of the need for conversion in unmistakable terms. As men and women are born into the world, and grow up, they live lives which are *alienated* from God (*Col. 1:21*), that is to say, they are morally and spiritually separated from God, apart from Him. Although they are made in the image of God (*Gen. 1:27*) and for His fellowship and service, they have departed from Him and so their lives are a living death. For although by God's goodness they retain the powers and abilities with which they were created, and in this sense have not become de-humanised, yet the focus of these gifts and powers is not towards God the giver but on themselves and others in opposition to God. The evidence of this death is seen in the basic irreligion of men and women, in the fact that they do not recognise an allegiance to God but attempt to evade His claims, in their actions of malice and hatred towards their fellow men, in social upheaval and in the witness of a bad conscience. It is true that the worst social effects are often, though not always, mitigated by the effects of culture and education. But the basic fact is that this rupture of the relationship between God and men made in the image of God is a *death* – a condition of separation from God, a breakdown of trust, an apathy or antagonism. It is a condition which can only be met by the breath of new spiritual life breathed at the command of God.

This is why the Christian church if she is faithful to her task does not ask people to be better or call upon them to turn over a new leaf or merely engage in efforts to alleviate human distress or to better the conditions of human life. Such advice even though it is well-intentioned is misplaced because it proceeds from a wrong or superficial diagnosis of the situation. To ask people to behave better, and to provide moral inspiration and instruction for them, presupposes they *can* behave better, and that they *want* to behave better, and that the only problem is that people are ignorant or weak-willed.

But this is the very thing that cannot be presupposed or taken for granted. The basic need is not for additional information or moral motivation but for the restoration with Almighty God of a relationship of love and trust and obedience which has been broken, and which can only be restored by the power of God, life from God, dispensed to needy men and women who come to Him at His own summons.

It is unfortunate that the word 'humanism' has come to be almost exclusively associated with modern secular humanism. For the Christian church exists to bear witness to humanism, not the humanism which sees men and women as the centre of the universe, which denies the existence of God and regards the prospect of life after death as wishful thinking, but the humanism which recognises that mankind was originally created in the image of God. This true humanism lies in the restoration of that image which has been lost due to human sin and rebellion against God. The Christian church does not exist to dehumanise men and women but to call them back to their true humanity, to a restoration in them of the divine image (*Col. 3:10*). And this restoration requires the conversion of the individual, his reorientation into the knowledge and service of God-in-Christ. Man's humanity, his nature, finds fulfilment not in the service of himself apart from God nor even in the service of other people apart from God but in the service of God Himself. From that basic relationship to God all other proper relationships follow.

This book is about Christian conversion, the beginnings of new life in Christ. To be more precise it is about the spiritual and theological framework of such conversion. But it is not offered as a description of the conscious experiences of conversion, of their varieties, stages, and durations. It is about the framework within which such experiences are to be interpreted and understood. More specifically still it is concerned with the various possibilities which face a person when the Christian message begins to gain a favourable hearing. As the gospel is preached and people pay attention to it, what is, or what might be, going on in their souls? How are they to understand what is going on?

This framework of understanding is vital, for Christian conversion is not simply a 'religious experience' of the sort which might be induced by drugs, or loud music, or by a walk through the countryside. Rather, the experience of Christian conversion is only intelligible as such when understood within the appropriate spiritual and theological framework. A simple illustration may help here. The fear of losing one's job is a very different sort of fear from the fear of losing one's car keys. What makes them different is that the fear in each case has a different object. In similar fashion, the elements of Christian conversion are not simply a collection of feelings or experiences, religious sensations, but they are elements set within a framework of understanding and belief about God, the person himself and the world around him.

This fact about the character of Christian experience is one of the reasons why it is impossible to think of the various major religions of the world – Christianity, Islam, Buddhism and so forth – as each agreeing in a common core of religious experience and differing only in the different interpretations which each has built around this common foundation. For it is not that the religious experience of the Buddhist is the same as that of the Christian, as two identical suits might be wrapped in different coloured wrapping paper. Rather, what *counts* as an experience of the grace of God for the Christian depends upon his understanding of that experience, the beliefs which support it and interpret it. For example, there cannot be an experience of saving grace according to the Christian gospel unless there is, as an aspect of it, the experience of conviction of sin and of penitence for sin. These are not detachable from the experience but are an integral part of it. An experience which lacked these features would not be the same *kind* of experience as one which possessed them, and it would not be a true Christian conversion.

The Christian rightly views with alarm attempts made within the Christian church to 'reinterpret' Christian experience. If the recognition of guilt before God is said to be 'nothing but' a feeling of personal or social inadequacy, or if it is to be 'explained' by reference to the strains of a strict upbringing, the result is not a better self-understanding but complete confusion. For if the experience of knowing oneself to be guilty before God on account of sin is explained away in this fashion then what is left is not a better understanding of one's experience and so a better understanding of oneself but a different experience altogether. The Christian's self-understanding, his identity as a Christian, is thus bound up with understanding what has happened to him in conversion. So it is not a light thing when it is held that, for example, all references to conviction of sin in conversion are 'legalism' and ought to be expunged. These matters will be taken up in a later chapter.

In the attempt in what follows to set out the spiritual and theological framework of Christian conversion three specific assumptions will be made. These will not be argued for, but some of their implications will be taken up in the ensuing chapters.

In the first place Christian conversion is the work of

God. It is necessary to emphasise this in view of the widespread misunderstanding. To say it is God's work is to say that the soul is passive, in a state of spiritual death, until the gift of regenerating grace is imparted by God. The New Testament makes this plain by the strong and clear way in which it invites us to think of conversion. Conversion is creation (*2 Cor. 4:6,7*) where the model is clearly the divine creation of the universe out of nothing. Conversion is also resurrection (*Eph. 2:5*), the raising of a dead soul to life again, as Christ was raised from the dead. But perhaps the most dominant thought-model of all in the New Testament is that of the new birth, in which the New Testament echoes the Old (*1 Pet. 1:23; Jas. 1:18; Ezek. 37*).

The New Testament has two lines of thought on how the new birth is brought about. It is the work of the Holy Spirit of God. In Christ's well-known conversation with Nicodemus (*John 3*) the new birth is referred to as being 'born of the spirit'. The new birth is utterly distinct from natural birth (*John 1:13*) and is brought about by the immediate influence of God upon the soul, creating new dispositions – new beliefs, new intentions and new desires. Christ emphasises that such work of the Spirit is at God's own disposal, for the Spirit is God's Spirit, and that it is mysterious, not fully fathomable by human reasoning or inquiry.

But the New Testament also teaches that the new birth is brought about by the word of God (*1 Pet. 1:23*), the word of the Lord (*1 Pet. 1:25*), the gospel, (*1 Pet. 1:25*), the word of truth (*Jas. 1:18*). The indispensable agent in conversion is God's revealed truth, the good news which centres in the provision of God's Son as a sacrifice for sin through which sinners are reconciled to God. This emphasis upon the word of God is also in effect an emphasis upon the mind of man, for the word of God does

not work in the soul by magic, but as it is understood and
believed (*Rom. 10:14*).

Needless to say these two lines of thought are not at
odds with each other. There is no contradiction here nor
even the slightest tension. Word and Spirit combine
together in the work of the new birth, in bringing men and
women to repentance and saving faith in Christ. Without
the Spirit the word of God is without effect. It is
disregarded or undervalued. It is given no higher authority than the words of men. Its message and thrust are not
appreciated, its relevance is undiscerned. Without the
Spirit, people *see*, but do not *perceive* (*Acts 28:26*). At the
same time without the word of God the work of the Spirit
would be similarly inefficacious because there would be no
message from God to be understood and to be believed. As
Christ testified, it is the work of the Spirit to take the
gospel of Christ and to 'reveal' it to hitherto darkened
minds and consciences (*John 16:13–16*).

The way in which word and Spirit combine in the work
of conversion is nowhere better expressed than in the New
Testament teaching on *calling*. Believers are called by
grace. To call someone involves the use of language – they
are personally addressed. Moreover in the New Testament such a call is effective in securing a response of faith
and penitence. It is not merely an indiscriminate call as
when the gospel is preached but it brings about a response
in the one called. What makes it effective? The fact that it
is the call of God by His Spirit in and through the word
(*Rom. 1:6, 9:11; 1 Cor. 1:9; Eph. 4:4*).

While at the onset of conversion the soul is passive the
soul does not remain passive. The effect of the work of
God in the soul is not to bypass or override its various
powers but to bring them to life and to sustain them in that
life. The Holy Spirit gives repentance and faith (*2 Tim.
2:25; Eph. 2:8*), but this is not the same thing as saying

that the Holy Spirit repents or believes. The faith and penitence is the disposition of the sinner, produced in him by the work of the Spirit. In giving such a disposition the Spirit works in a way which is entirely in harmony with the persons concerned in that they are not compelled by the Spirit to do things against their will or which they regard as unreasonable but rather they are made willing and made to see the appropriateness of their actions. This implantation of spiritual life – regeneration – leads invariably to repentance and saving faith and the whole may be described as the effectual call of God. This is the first specific assumption which is presupposed in what is to follow.

The second assumption is that conversion is by means of God's truth. As was noted, according to the New Testament word and Spirit combine together in the work of conversion. Each is necessary and together they are sufficient. The word is not some magical formula, a spell or an incantation, it is God's truth. It is as men and women receive this truth, as they understand it, that the Holy Spirit disposes them to believe it and to place their trust in the Saviour whose power to deliver from sin is the focal point of that truth. This is another way in which God, in conversion, works in people in a way which is wholly consistent with their personalities. Nothing is more familiar to us than reading or hearing what people have to say and understanding them. The whole of our lives together in families and communities is based upon such understanding. So it is in conversion. It is as the word of God is read or heard, in private Bible-reading or in preaching or in debate and discussion, that God the Holy Spirit imparts an understanding of it and con-fidence in it. Such understanding is not mystical. There is no 'hidden' meaning of Scripture which is available only to a select few. It is the open, public and natural meaning of Scripture that the Holy Spirit uses. Through His guidance the various pieces of divine revelation are put together, like the pieces of a jig-saw puzzle, until the whole makes sense and its relevance to the personal needs of the individual is made clear and the person in question comes to place himself under the authority of the word of God.

To say that this is the work of the Holy Spirit is not to say that the person always recognises it to be such. No one can see without the proper functioning of the optic nerve but one does not have to be aware of this fact in order to see. A person who knows nothing about the working of the human eye may still see perfectly well. In a similar way a person may not be aware that the Holy Spirit is working within him. For the work of the Holy Spirit is known through its effects – a desire for knowledge of the word of God, conviction of sin, faith in Christ and penitence before God. And these effects might be present in someone who is unaware that they are the work of God's Spirit in him.

So in conversion God does not work in a way which is unrelated to the mind. Conversion does not require intellectual paralysis or suicide. It cannot take place when the mind is asleep, or drugged, or otherwise disengaged. Rather it is through the mind's understanding of God's truth and it is as that understanding takes place that God the Holy Spirit is pleased to implant new life. In this sense conversion is 'reasonable'; it involves the use of the mind, the reason.

So although the world at large may provide men with some small inkling of God and of His ways and His purposes, they depend chiefly upon what God has been pleased to do in human history and on what He has been pleased to tell them. They depend upon what God has revealed about and through His Son Jesus Christ. In a similar way, although a person's conscience alone may tell him something of his predicament in relation to God, he depends for the knowledge of the full extent of his need on what God has been pleased to tell him in Holy Scripture.

Truths about God, and truths about ourselves. Conversion is not a mere psychological manipulation. It is not brainwashing or a confidence trick. It is not something which takes place in a particular culture or climate of thought, in the twentieth century but not in the tenth, or among North Americans but not among the Matabele. It is not something which may be 'valid for me but not valid for you'. It is based upon truth.

The third assumption to be made is that in the work of conversion the Holy Spirit uses both the law and the gospel. In using God's revealed truth to bring men to conversion the Holy Spirit *diagnoses* the need of men, and specifies the *remedy*. The rupture which has taken place in the relationship between God and men is moral and spiritual. The effects of this rupture are widespread throughout human society and culture. But the cause is personal, both moral and spiritual. It follows that in conversion the Holy Spirit brings to the attention of men and women through the Scriptures their plight and need, their moral calamity and the danger of their condition.

That calamity is only fully measured by the law, God's law. Mankind is made in the image of God and this means that he was made for the service of God in a proper moral relationship with Him, a relationship of thankful obedience. Mankind was not created in a moral vacuum. How far people have fallen away from that original relationship is to be measured not by their feelings or by what seems reasonable or by the prevailing social standards but by God's law as this is revealed in the Decalogue, in the life and teaching of Christ, and in the teaching of the apostles. It is a law of love, concerned both with our relationship to God and to other men and reaching not only to outward, observable actions but to hidden motives and intentions. Judged by this standard, mankind is in a state of rebellion against God.

It is for such people that the gospel of God's love and mercy in the giving up of His Son to death is provided. The cross of Christ is not simply a general symbol of the love of God for men or an example of self-giving love to be imitated or an inspiring ideal. It is God's remedial action for the plight of men, God's remedy for law-breakers, God's means of restoring men and women to their true relationship with Him. God, the offended Creator, Himself provides the remedy in the giving of His Son. And men and women begin consciously to benefit from that remedy when, forsaking all attempts at gaining the favour of God, they trust Christ and so die with Him, are raised with Him, and share His life and destiny.

Wherever this message gains a hearing there is division. Some reject it as being foolish and unworthy of them, even degrading and debasing. Others respond more favourably. This book is about those who are beginning to respond favourably to the gospel. It has to do with the elements, the structural principles, of Christian conversion. In particular it has to do with the question of how a person who is inclined to respond favourably to the gospel message may be helped to recognise whether or not God is truly at work in him. Three specific alternative possibilities will be examined. The first possibility is that such a person is experiencing conviction of sin but not true penitence. The second possibility is that such a person is penitent but for the wrong reasons. And the third possibility is that such a person has true faith in Christ and penitence toward God. Having looked at these three possibilities attention will be given to some objections which have been brought against such an understanding of conversion. The final chapter is devoted to some of the wider implications of this understanding of conversion for the life of the Christian church.

1 : *Conviction without Confession*

Christian conversion comes about at the initiative of God for it depends upon the gift of spiritual life. The precise time when this life is received is not something which a person can be aware of, because it occurs below the level of self-awareness. But, combined with an understanding of the word of God, it gives rise to a distinctive experience – to changes in belief and emotion and behaviour. Or, to be more precise, it gives rise to an experience with a distinctive structure. This qualification is important. The experiences of conversion are infinitely varied but they all have the same structure. The order, intensity and duration of particular experiences of conversion and the circumstances in which they are set may differ from person to person, but the elements of the experience are the same. This is not peculiar to conversion or to religious experience. No two football games or illnesses or courtships are the same. But this does not mean that just *anything* could count as a football game or that a football game could be confused with a courtship. Though each is varied in this way yet they have a distinctive structure of belief, a distinctive point, perhaps distinctive rules and effects.

Consider these two accounts given by different Christians of their own conversion. During an intense experience of contrition for his sins, Augustine

> heard from a neighbouring house a voice, as of a boy or girl, I know not, chanting, and oft repeating, 'Take up

and read; take up and read'. Instantly, my countenance altered, I began to think most intently, whether children were wont in any kind of play to sing such words: nor could I remember ever to have heard the like. So checking the torrent of my tears, I arose; interpreting it to be no other than a command from God to open the book and read the first chapter I should find . . . I seized, opened, and in silence read that passage, on which my eyes first fell: *Not in rioting and drunkenness, not in chambering and wantonness, not in strife and envying: but put ye on the Lord Jesus Christ, and make not provision for the flesh*, in concupiscence. No further would I read; nor needed I: for instantly at the end of this sentence, by a light as it were of serenity infused into my heart, all the darkness of doubt vanished away.

In his booklet, *A Self-portrait* the Anglican leader of the last century, J. C. Ryle, remarked that:

The circumstances which led to a complete change in my character were very many and very various, and I think it right to mention them. It was not a sudden immediate change but very gradual. I cannot trace it to any one person, or any one event or thing, but to a singular variety of persons and things. In all of them I believe now the Holy Ghost was working, though I did not know it at the time.

These are, clearly, two very different experiences. But they are both cases of conversion. Such variety of experience, recorded throughout the history of the church, is to be found already in Scripture. The experience of Zacchæus (*Luke 19:1–10*) is different from that of Saul of Tarsus (*Acts 9:12–22*), that of Lydia (*Acts 16:14*) is different from the experience of Nathanael (*John 1:45–51*).

Yet for all this variety it is clear that not *anything* counts as a conversion. What, then, are its elements? In the remainder of this chapter and in the next two an attempt will be made to look in detail at this question. But it needs to be stressed at the beginning that this will be an examination of the *elements* of conversion, its basic structure, and not of the successive stages of conversion. Some of the dangers of treating the elements as if they were stages will be looked at in chapter four.

CONVICTION

Conversion is the deepest of all changes, a change in a person's relationship to God, his Creator and Lord. This relationship is a moral one, one of obligation to God to keep His law. Man's plight and his need for conversion arises from his wilful refusal to keep that law and the moral breakdown that has followed. A person's relationship to God is unique, for no one else occupies or could occupy God's position as Creator. It is to misunderstand that relationship to think of it as one of friendship like a human friendship. It is one of law yet not of the abstract, impersonal law of a modern legal system, but of what might be called personal law, the law of God the Creator and Upholder of all things, the One who in virtue of His position has the right to command.

Even in their rebellion against God men still retain their character as moral beings. It is not as if rebellion has transformed men into mere animals or into bits of machinery. They retain their moral agency and even, so the Bible assures us, some faint inkling of God and of His ways, so much so that the rebellion may express itself not only in indifference to God, but in hostility to Him, even to a half-understood hostility which may show itself in hostility to goodness in any of its various guises. Men are often hostile to God's law even when God's existence is denied.

The fact that men retain their character as moral beings

and have not become in their rebellion against God mere animals or robots is also revealed when they experience remorse or regret at their actions. They have a conscience, a moral sense, which is part of the divine image in them. They judge certain matters to be right, other matters to be wrong or even morally outrageous. They condemn others, and they also condemn themselves.

Paul reminds us in Romans that these reactions take place in every human being and culture. They are not restricted to those people who have had the benefit of a Christian upbringing. Even those without such an upbringing often do 'by nature' the things contained in the law (*Rom. 2:14*). For example they respect other people's property, they refrain from killing and from adultery, and they are helpful to their neighbours. And, Paul continues, their conscience is at work, either accusing them, or excusing them (*Rom. 2:15*); accusing them when they act against the moral principles which they adhere to and excusing them (i.e. vindicating them) when they believe themselves to act in accordance with their moral principles.

Having a bad conscience about certain things and a good conscience about other things is a universal fact of life. Men invariably judge some things to be morally wrong and other things to be morally right. Part of God's work in conversion is to convince men that certain of the things that they do, or want to do but cannot bring themselves to do, are against the law of God, and also that they omit to do many of the things that God requires of them. The Holy Spirit not only convinces such people that they do certain things that are wrong and omit to do what is right but He also convinces people that such corrupt behaviour springs from a corrupt source. He shows a person that his own innermost desires and intentions which give rise to his actions are not in

[25]

accordance with the will of God.

But to say that in conversion the Holy Spirit convinces people of their sin is not to say that *anything* which people come to think of as wrong, and as being against the law of God, is in fact so or to say that every such evaluation is the result of the convincing work of the Holy Spirit. Suppose a person comes to think that it is morally wrong to eat meat or to go abroad for his holidays or to have coal fires in the house. Such convictions cannot be the result of the operation of the Holy Spirit in conversion. Why not? Because such principles form no part of the law of God. It is no part of God's requirement of men and women made in His image that they do not eat meat or have their holidays in England or heat their homes without using coal. So that not everything which a person may feel guilty about is true guilt before God. It is necessary to distinguish between true guilt and guilt-feelings. How is this to be done?

It was stressed in the Introduction that in conversion God's word and Spirit combine together and here is a vivid illustration of how they operate conjointly. The word of God is necessary to inform people of what the standards of righteousness are and by how much they fail to keep to those standards. It is important to be clear about this at the present time for people are often 'hung up' over matters which are simply superstitious or traditional and have nothing to do with the law of God. At the same time there is a widespread feeling that all moral rules or laws are simply subjective or relative to a culture. Stealing is wrong, it is said, not because stealing *is* wrong but because 'we have decided' to regard stealing as wrong.

But according to Scripture there are objective standards of right and wrong, objective not because God has laid them down in an arbitrary or tyrannical manner but because they correspond to His nature and are related to human welfare and well-being. In the obedience to God's commandments lies not only the honouring of God, but human flourishing, the flourishing of those who are made in the image of God.

By what route does the conviction of sin come about? Here it is important not to be dogmatic. The temptation to lay down certain steps or stages must be resisted. But it may be helpful to distinguish between various possibilities. It has already been seen that awareness of wrongdoing is a universal human experience. The conviction of sin, the awareness that wrongdoing is an offence against God, is often continuous with such experience. A person living in a largely secular or pagan environment takes his standards of morality either from a traditional religion or from secular humanism. He may have a 'conscience' about many matters and may attempt to reform his life accordingly. In this situation the word of God can come to a person, through hearing preaching or reading, and reform and 'fill out' that person's moral principles. The Holy Spirit may thus convince that person that when his conduct is assessed by biblical standards he is guilty before God.

Another person may grow up with the knowledge of the word of God and be to some extent under its influence. The process of conviction may in his case take the form of his eyes being 'opened' to the recognition of his guilt, realising that his own responsibility to God is not confined to the actions seen by others but extends to what is private and invisible, his undisclosed thoughts and feelings. He is convinced that in relation to God's standards he is guilty and under judgment.

In such situations the word of God and the Spirit of God combine together. But what part of the word of God? Here again it is wise not to be too dogmatic. Yet it is possible to conceive of two broad aspects of the word of God which may figure in the work of conviction. There is, firstly, that aspect of the word of God which stresses the demand of God, the law of God. This may be recognised in the Ten Commandments or in the teaching of Christ on the law, perhaps in those aspects of the Sermon on the Mount which stress that the law has to do not only with conduct, but with inner desire and motivation. Or it may be seen in the teaching of the apostles about the law, set in the context of the need to re-form and regulate the lives of the early Christians many of whom had come out of a pagan background. In one or other of these direct ways the Holy Spirit may take some aspect of the law of God and convince a person of his own guilt before God as a law-breaker.

But it is possible to think of a less direct route by which someone may be convinced of his sin. The life and ministry of Jesus Christ and especially His death as these are properly understood provide an indirect means of understanding the law of God and what it implies. For the life of Jesus Christ was sinless (*Heb. 7:26*) and He provided a living embodiment of the law of God. And so recognising the holy character of Jesus provides a measure of a person's own sinfulness and may lead to the conviction of sin. This happened to Peter when he realised his own sinfulness while in the presence of Christ (*Luke 5:8*).

To understand the significance of the death of Jesus is to gain the deepest insight into the character and depth of the law of God. For Jesus came to pay the penalty of the breaking of divine law by sinners, to satisfy divine justice and so remove their guilt. The depth and extent of the divine response to sin is a measure of the seriousness of sin. If the bearing away of sin requires the death of the eternal Son of God made flesh, what an offence sin must be to God! Christ is not only an example of sinlessness, therefore, but also His death is the best measure of what human sinfulness means in God's sight. If

There was no other good enough
To pay the price of sin

this shows not only the extent of the love of God but also the depth of the need which called forth that love. The two are related in that the extent of the divine love reveals the sinfulness of sin while the sinfulness of sin shows the depth and extent of the divine love.

So it would be a mistake rigidly to divide the word of God into 'the law' and 'the gospel' and to suppose that neither is involved with the other and that the church's proclamation of human need involves certain selected texts or isolated parts of the Scripture while the preaching of the gospel involves other selected and isolated parts. Peter was convinced of his sin by the power and grace of the Saviour and the thief on the cross by our Lord's innocent suffering (*Luke 23:39–41*). The law interprets the gospel. The gospel cannot be understood without the law.

What, then, is conviction of sin? A person is convinced of sin when he recognises that he is a transgressor of God's law and that he deserves the judgment of God. This is one element, one ingredient, in true Christian conversion. Some people may be separately aware of this conviction, while in the case of others, it may be indistinguishable from the other elements, part of one complex conversion experience.

There are a number of instances in Scripture where conviction of sin may be identified as a separate phase of awareness. One prominent example is the reaction of many Jews to Peter's preaching on the Day of Pentecost when the Holy Spirit was 'poured out' upon the early church. After witnessing the strange phenomenon in which groups of Jews from various parts of the world heard the mighty works of God proclaimed each in their own native language, Peter addresses the Jews. He reminds them that what was happening came to pass in accordance with the words of Old Testament prophecy and then spoke to them directly. The thrust of his preaching was that the Jesus whom they had wickedly crucified had been raised up by God, also in accordance with the prophecies of the Old Testament, and that God had made Jesus the Lord Christ, the Judge of all. It was this Christ, the Christ whom they had crucified, who had sent the Holy Spirit whose influence they were now witnessing (*Acts 2:14-36*).

When the Jews heard this 'they were pricked in their heart' (*v. 37*). What does this mean? In Scripture the word translated 'heart', both in the Old Testament and in the New, signifies the inner self or personality, including the conscience. The Jews became convinced that what Peter was saying was true. They realised that although they thought that they had handed over a blasphemer to the Roman authorities they were in fact guilty of crucifying God's Anointed. As they had been His enemies, were they not now to expect that He would be their enemy?

Their consciences were stricken. This was not merely an emotional impulse, a sudden and irrational feeling. Their consciences were affected because of what they had suddenly realised, what they had come to believe. They had come to believe that they were guilty, that they had broken God's law. In slaying the innocent, the plain, objective fact of the matter was that they were guilty and their consciences registered this fact. This prompted them to cry out in bewilderment and despair, and Peter, in reply, points them to the Saviour. The one whom they had crucified, the Anointed of God, the Judge of all, is the Saviour of sinners.

In other cases in Scripture the conviction of sin is not a separately identifiable phase of experience but its presence may be inferred. For example, Jesus called Zacchæus down from the tree into which he had climbed in order to get a better view of the Saviour's progress through Jericho. Suddenly, apparently without warning, Jesus invited Himself to Zacchæus' house. Jesus' behaviour immediately prompted a reaction. What justification was there for Him to stay with Zacchæus, for Zacchæus had become rich through the exploitation of others? Zacchæus heard of this and responded by telling Jesus, 'Lord, the half of my goods I give to the poor; and if I have taken anything from any man by false accusation, I restore him fourfold' (*Luke 19:8*).

What is to be made of this? At first sight it may seem as if Zacchæus is bent on justifying himself. But this would be to misunderstand what had happened. Zacchæus was indicating the results of his penitence. He had climbed the tree not merely out of curiosity but because, as a penitent extortioner, he needed the Saviour. Perhaps his penitence was recent. News of it was not generally known. But it was known to Jesus.

How is this known? Because of what Jesus said to him in reply: 'This day is salvation come to this house, forsomuch as he also is a son of Abraham. For the Son of man is come to seek and to save that which was lost' (*vv. 9, 10*). In Jesus' eyes Zacchæus was one of the lost. Though made rich through extortion salvation had come to him, and the evidence of his lostness was that he had forsaken his injustice and his covetousness – as was shown by his willingness to make restitution – and had recognised his need for salvation.

There is no distinct phase of Zacchæus' experience which can be identified as a time of conviction of sin. But the fact that he was convinced of his sin can be seen from his behaviour. The genuineness of his penitence was shown by the recognition of his guilt and his refusal to cover it up.

So conviction of sin, whether it is a distinct phase of experience or an element in a more complex experience which it is difficult to identify separately, is an essential ingredient or strand in conversion. It is the product of the Holy Spirit enlightening the mind to recognise the justice of God's law and showing to the sinner that he has broken it and is thus guilty before God.

IS CONVICTION ENOUGH?

Conviction of sin is a necessary element in Christian conversion, but is it sufficient? How is this question to be decided? The danger is that the question will be answered more by tradition or by a person's own preferences or ideals than by the truth. It is tempting to impose one's own model of what Christian conversion is or should be, but this temptation must be resisted.

Scripture provides vivid cases of people who have been convinced of their sin but who have not been truly converted, or at least were not properly converted as far as we can tell. Among numerous instances that could be cited two examples will be examined.

(a) *Christ and the rich young ruler (Matt. 19:16–22)*. The details of this story are familiar enough. Christ is approached by a rich young ruler who, no doubt prompted by Christ's own teaching, had become concerned about his relationship with God. He asks, 'What must I do to inherit eternal life?' It is clear from this question that the man thought of eternal life as something which he had to gain or to attain to by his own efforts. The emphasis of his question is upon his willingness to do whatever was necessary. The only problem as far as he was concerned was that he did not know what to do. He thought that all he needed was the right information. His question showed both personal concern and self-sufficiency.·

Christ takes the person's question with great seriousness and points him to the law. 'If thou wilt enter into life, keep the commandments' (*v. 17*). Christ presented him with God's claims through His law, emphasising that the law is God's law ('There is none good but one, that is, God: but if thou wilt enter into life, keep the commandments'). Christ's reaction here shows, incidentally, that it is a serious distortion to suppose that He substituted teaching about divine love for the Old Testament teaching about the law. Throughout His ministry, in, for example, the Sermon on the Mount (*Matt. 5–7*), in questions about which was the greatest commandment (*Matt. 22:35–40*), and here in His conversation with the rich young ruler, Christ is emphatic that love is not opposed to law, but rather that love expresses and is expressed by the law.

When in response to a further question Jesus spells out the claims of the moral law in detail the young man replies, 'All these have I kept from my youth up: what lack I yet?' (*v. 20*). The question reveals the tension in his life. He was confident that he had kept the commandments, and yet he was aware of a continuing need. But he did not truly know himself. For though he thought he had kept the commandments, in fact he had not. If he had truly kept the commandments what reason was there to ask Christ 'What lack I yet?'

Christ's reply to *this* question, His advice to the man, 'If thou wilt be perfect, go and sell that thou hast, and give to the poor', touches upon the source of his sin and need, namely, his covetousness. (It is interesting that when Christ spelled out the detail of the moral law to him He omitted to mention the commandment, 'Thou shalt not covet'.)

[33]

The young man left Christ sorrowful. Why was this? Because 'he had great possessions' (*v. 22*). Yet it was not simply the fact that he was rich but because he had gained or was holding on to his riches through covetousness. He was sorrowful because he was convinced of his covetousness and yet wished to continue to indulge it.

Here is a person who has a desire for eternal life and who recognises that in his present circumstances he will not attain it. To begin with he has a sense of his need, but a need that is vague and hard to pinpoint. As a result of his conversation with Christ he comes to recognise more precisely what his need is – to be rid of his covetousness and to follow Christ. In realising this he also is brought to see a further thing, that keeping the law is not merely a matter of behaviour but that the law extends to a person's inner, private state. Covetousness may never reveal itself at all, or may never reveal itself in distinctive actions, and yet the law forbids it. The rich young ruler was convinced of his need, and this made him sorrowful. He was sorrowful as well at the thought of having to part with his possessions. Yet in spite of his sorrow he did not do as Christ advised him. He left Christ, and kept his possessions.

(b) *Felix (Acts 24)*. Paul appeared twice before Felix. On the first occasion, when he was accused by Tertullus speaking on behalf of the Jews, Paul defended himself and Felix deferred judgment until Lysias arrived (*Acts 24:22*), keeping Paul meanwhile under fairly liberal house-arrest (*v. 23*). A few days afterwards Felix sent for Paul again to hear about the Christian gospel from him (*v. 24*). In the course of his preaching Paul 'reasoned of righteousness, temperance and judgment to come', as he had done, for example, while preaching at Athens (*Acts 17:31*). Felix trembled when he heard what Paul said and sent him away. He saw Paul on several occasions afterwards, but only in the hope that Paul would bribe him in order to obtain release (*v. 26*).

When Paul reasoned about righteousness, temperance and judgment to come, what was he reasoning about? It is clear that this was not a purely abstract discourse. Paul was in deadly earnest. When he talked about righteousness he did not mean what passed for righteousness in Felix's circle of friends but divine righteousness, the righteousness of God, the need to be righteous before God. And when he spoke of temperance he meant that standard of conduct which was in accordance with the will of God. And he spoke of these things in the light of a certain future judgment and as a herald of 'the faith in Christ', a preacher of God's righteousness as it is freely offered to sinners in Jesus Christ.

When he heard this, Felix did not brush it aside as Jewish nonsense. He trembled. And he must have trembled because he believed or was inclined to believe what Paul was saying. For a short while, perhaps only for a few minutes, Felix became convinced that there was a judgment to come and that righteousness was needed to avert it. And then – it seems, very quickly – he indicated to Paul that he had heard enough and had him ushered out of his presence (*v. 25*).

Felix was impressed by the word of God. He realised, at least fleetingly, his own shortcomings when measured against the righteousness of God. He recognised these matters not as speculative possibilities but as truths which made him tremble. But then he put them to one side. His old nature reasserted itself. He became interested only in the money which he could make out of having Paul released.

Felix was convinced that he would be judged by God. He was convinced of his sins. And yet as his subsequent behaviour very quickly shows, he was not converted. He reverted to his old self.

WHAT WAS THE MATTER?

Both the rich young ruler and Felix recognised the fact of God's law and of its claims upon them. They were not caught up in some vague emotional experience. In the case of the rich young ruler the recognition was explicit and direct. He knew the law as the law, within the setting of the Jewish nation; he endeavoured to keep it but recognised that he still lacked something. It is likely that Felix did not recognise the law of God in this formal sense. We cannot be sure. Perhaps he did. It depends upon what Paul said or upon Felix's general knowledge.

But a person does not need to have a formal and explicit acquaintance with the Ten Commandments, or with the teaching of Christ, in order to know the law. His knowledge of the law may be imperfect and half-formed and yet he may be said to be aware of it because he recognises certain rules or principles or laws as carrying the authority of God. So a person may recognise that it is against God's will to steal, or to blaspheme, even though he may be ignorant of the rest of God's law. This may have been true of Felix when Paul reasoned about righteousness, temperance and judgment to come.

Both Felix and the rich young ruler recognised their personal responsibility to God. They regarded the law of God not in an abstract or theoretical way, but believed themselves to be personally accountable to God for breaking it. The rich young ruler had a strong desire to keep the law in order to gain eternal life. He believed that gaining eternal life depended upon his behaviour while at the same time recognising that he lacked something. He recognised the authority of Jesus' teaching and his failure to follow Jesus made him sorrowful. All this suggests a person who treated his own responsibility before God with great seriousness as something which had occupied him all his life.

Felix, by contrast, may only have been stirred to a recognition of his accountability to God on one occasion. But when he trembled at the prospect of judgment this can only have been because he believed himself to lack the righteousness of God of which Paul spoke. This lack was not something which Felix shrugged off casually but which he felt acutely. He recognised, if only for a few moments, the truth about himself before God, and this made him anxious, so much so that it seems that he was extremely uncomfortable in Paul's presence. But this anxiety was soon submerged in his more general concern for money.

What, then, was the matter in these cases? What was missing? The trouble was not with the fact of sorrow and concern but with the sort of sorrow and concern that it was. Although each recognised the law of God, his own obligation to it, and his failure to keep it, the recognition of this failure prompted in them both an inappropriate response. The rich young ruler was sorrowful. While his sorrow was due to a recognition of his particular sin, his covetousness, yet his sorrow was not *on account of* his sin. Rather he was sorrowful at the thought that if he followed Jesus he would have to give his wealth away. His property was central to his life. It was what consumed him. To be asked to part with it, to give it away, filled him with sorrow.

In the case of Felix, while he trembled at the mention of the judgment to come, it seems that he trembled not because of a recognition of his own sin before God but simply at the idea of judgment. He did not like the idea of judgment, and Paul was so persuasive and so convincing about it in his reasoning that for a few moments Felix became convinced that he faced divine judgment. Yet this did not lead him to forsake his sins but to dismiss Paul from his presence.

SOME CONCLUSIONS

From these two cases it is possible to draw some general conclusions about the nature of true conversion. Such conversion involves not merely the personal recognition of sin but conviction of sin *for the right reasons*. All other conviction of sin is likely to prove temporary and abortive. True conviction involves a person recognising certain unwelcome truths about himself, that in relation to the law of God he is a law-breaker and that he has offended God. A person must form a correct estimate of himself in his relation to God, involving the awareness that he is a sinner in God's sight. But more than this, conviction involves an awareness of what sin is in God's sight coupled with a resolve to hate it and to forsake it because it is displeasing to God. Although Felix and the rich young ruler had become convinced of their sin, there is no evidence that their attitude to their sin had fundamentally changed.

The difference between the two sorts of conviction of sin can be illustrated as follows. Suppose that someone is accused of stealing and comes to recognise that he has in fact stolen. This realisation or the disgrace of being found out may be a profound shock to him. Yet his attitude to his behaviour need not have undergone any fundamental change. The fact that his behaviour is condemned may upset him but he may still wish to continue to steal and to get away with whatever he can. For true conviction of sin there must not only be a changed belief as to a person's relationship to God, an awareness of his short-coming, but there must also be a changed judgment about the nature of the offence in question. A person must recognise his own sin for what it is and hate it.

Does that mean that the thought of final judgment must play no part in the true conviction of sin? By no means! Final judgment is to be feared because it is separation from God.

The possibility of conviction without confession is what each person must face as he hears the Christian gospel, gains some knowledge of God's revelation, and is swayed by its message – the possibility that he will be convinced of his sin but not turn from that sin in penitence. One possibility that a minister of the gospel faces as he preaches and exercises his pastoral office is that there will be men and women who will be impressed with what he says and show personal concern about the message and yet who will not respond to the gospel in repentance and faith.

Such people are not regenerate. They are not converted. Yet the definiteness of this fact does not mean that anyone can pass final judgment upon such people. For one thing, no one is in a position to say what will happen in the future. God's Spirit is sovereign in His work (*John 3:8*), and so that work cannot be directed, or anticipated. or predicted by man. Regenerating grace is given in accordance with the will of God. And the fact that a person has undergone a period of conviction of sin, even if it seems to be or has proved to be temporary, provides no conclusive evidence for supposing that God will never grant His regenerating grace to that person in the future. God often works in ways which are surprising, and the temptation to try to box Him in with theories of how and when He must work has to be resisted (*1 Cor. 1:26–9*).

A second reason for hesitancy in offering a definitive verdict on the spiritual condition of others is that often the most significant dimension of that condition is hidden or private and hence known only to God. This can be seen by reconsidering the account of the rich young ruler. As far as his outward and public behaviour is concerned he was exemplary. He kept the law. His deficiency lay in his covetousness, something which was 'inward', which was not generally known and which was only revealed publicly as a result of the Saviour's challenge to him to sell everything and give away the proceeds to the poor. To stress the importance of the inner self is not to say that lives are not dramatically changed as a result of the coming of regenerating grace – Zacchæus is a case of someone dramatically changed – but the extent of such a change will clearly depend upon how a person behaved before.

Another reason for reticence in passing judgment on the spiritual condition of men and women is that God's regenerating grace often has small beginnings. It would be harsh and insensitive to dismiss a person because he or she did not measure up to certain standards. What is hastily dismissed as a temporary phase, a superficial work, may turn out to be the beginnings of something deeper.

There is one healthy general rule which may be adopted. The New Testament's emphasis, when it is concerned with the reality or otherwise of spiritual work in a person, is not only on whether the person *has been* converted, but on whether he *is* converted. For if a person is converted, if he now gives evidence of regenerating grace, then it follows that he has been converted. But if he professes to be 'converted' and there is no evidence of present spiritual life then that profession is hollow. Ways of thinking about Christian experience which stress the need for a definite experience of conversion often encourage a person to look back to that experience for assurance. And slogans such as 'Once saved, always saved' encourage this as well because they invite a person to infer that if there was a period in his life when he made a definite profession of faith he must be saved now. But this is to get the biblical pattern of regeneration back to front. That pattern is: if a person is converted now, then he has been converted. Although the New Testament occasionally invites us to gain assurance from the past, especially during times of spiritual distress or pressure, it never does this in order to encourage or re-inforce complacency. The plain fact of the matter for the Christians to whom Peter wrote was not that they had been begotten again by the word of God, but that, at the time he wrote, they were begotten again (*1 Peter 2*).

DOES GOD TOY WITH MEN?

It may be thought that the fact that there can be conviction of sin without true repentance means that God toys with men. In order properly to understand this issue it is necessary to remember two principles. The first is that the experience of the conviction of sin is due to the operation of the Holy Spirit. Although there are purely natural promptings of conscience, yet the fact that a person recognises himself to be guilty before God is as a result of the work of the Holy Spirit upon him. Calvin, for example, stresses this in his comments on Felix's reaction to Paul's reasoning. He says that the conviction of Felix's conscience was due to the work of the Holy Spirit as foretold by Christ (*John 16:7–14*). The second principle is that Scripture teaches that there are cases of such conviction which are purely temporary and which are not the result of regenerating grace, as when a person is convicted of his sins but is not willing to turn away from his sins.

So it seems that there are activities of the Holy Spirit in the souls of men which are of a purely temporary nature. This is confirmed also by such passages as Hebrews 6 and also, perhaps, by Christ's parable of the sower. Faced with this clear biblical position some have been tempted to suppose that God treats some people as playthings, that He toys with them like a cat with a mouse, granting to them temporary influences of His Spirit without ever the intention of truly regenerating them and uniting them to Christ. And also, it is sometimes said, if there are temporary operations of the Spirit as distinct from His permanent operations in regeneration and true conversion, how is a person to know which is which? How is he to know whether he is experiencing the temporary or the permanent influences of the Holy Spirit?

How are these questions to be answered? By remembering the biblical pattern of conversion. Suppose that as he was listening to Paul and trembling Felix had said to himself 'these are only temporary convictions; God is playing with me'. If he had said this he would have had no warrant to believe that what he said was true, for there was no evidence that made it reasonable to believe it. The fact that God does sometimes grant temporary influences of His Spirit does not imply to anyone that his own experience is a case in point. Suppose, alternatively, that Felix had offered as evidence for the idea that the influences were temporary the fact that his experiences were of the character described earlier. Even this would provide no reason to conclude that God was dealing with him in a purely temporary fashion, because for all that he knew such influences might in due course be followed imperceptibly by the deeper, permanent, regenerating influences of God's Spirit. From the fact that a certain phase of God's work seems to bear the mark of being a temporary influence no one is warranted in concluding that this may not be preliminary to the granting of regenerating grace.

Suppose finally that after the encounter with Paul, when he had come to be more interested in money than in the judgment to come, Felix had reflected on his experience and concluded that it was a temporary influence of the Holy Spirit. Would he be warranted in concluding that God had merely been toying with him and that God had no concern to convert him by regenerating grace? Certainly not! For all Felix knew to the contrary (and perhaps it is fair to say for all that is known to the contrary about Felix) God might at some time subsequent to his encounter with Paul have come to him with regenerating grace and power. For all that is known to the contrary this may in fact have happened.

The important question to ask is not what is abstractly possible in such situations but what the person is warranted in believing about himself in relation to God's saving purposes. What do the evidence of his own experience and of what he knows of the promises and purposes of God in relation to people who are placed in a situation such as he is in warrant him in concluding?

It is true that the New Testament does indicate that there are situations in which a person, by his resolute and unremitting opposition to the gospel of grace, effectively rules himself out from that grace. This is clearly what Christ taught in His few words about the sin against the Holy Ghost (*Matt. 12:31*). And Hebrews 6 indicates that there are situations in which people who were once enlightened, if they fall away, will find it impossible to be renewed to repentance. For they have crucified the Son of God afresh and have put Him to an open shame. But such situations are exceptional and indicate resolute and unremitting hostility to the gospel. It may even be the case, as some interpret the passage, that the writer in Hebrews is holding out such possibilities as purely hypothetical in an effort to warn his readers against the danger of drawing back from their profession. It is the very knowledge of what the consequences of drawing back would be which prevents them from doing so.

But there is nevertheless the fact, suggested by the

[43]

biblical accounts of the rich young ruler, of Felix, and of others, that God does deal with certain people in such a way as to grant them the temporary influences of the Spirit. Why is this? Why is there no hard and fast, black and white distinction between those who have regenerating grace and those who do not have it? Why this shady, grey area? It is possible to think of possible explanations of this state of affairs. One reason might be that such cases are to act as warnings against complacency and false assurance among those who are truly regenerate (see, for example, how the writer to the Hebrews uses the account of the Old Testament Jews who fell in the wilderness to encourage his readers to watchfulness and fear, *Heb. 4:1*). But when all such reasons have been offered and examined the sovereignty of God must be recognised. These puzzles along with many other puzzles having to do with God's permission of evil and with the chequered history of the church on earth are locked in the inscrutable purposes of God. 'Even so, Father, for so it seemed good in thy sight' (*Matt. 11:26*) is the most apt commentary on such events.

STRANDS NOT STAGES

This chapter has been concerned with the fact that some people become aware of their sins, and nothing more, and with looking at some of the implications of that fact. One conclusion is that conviction of sin is one aspect or strand in conversion but it is not the only one. It is tempting to think of this *aspect* as a *stage*, the indispensable first stage in the conversion experience. And it is an undoubted fact that many have thought of the conviction of sin in this way. They have thought of it as a stage that must be gone through on the way to a truly saving experience of God's grace. First, conviction of sin, and then some time later, faith and repentance.

But this would be a mistake. It may be true that the experience of conviction of sin is the almost invariable forerunner of other experiences which together make up the experience of conversion. But to insist that this is and must be *the* invariable pattern of Christian experience is a mistake because it leads in the direction of legalism. Almost imperceptibly and often for the best of pastoral motives a pattern of thought is adopted which lays down conditions for the experience of God's saving grace. What begins as a description of experience ends up as a rule which says, in effect, that a person cannot be a Christian unless he has *first* experienced the conviction of sin. But then further questions rear their ugly heads. How long must be experience of conviction of sin? Minutes? Hours? Days? How intense must it be? How is that intensity to be measured? In terms of emotions? In terms of bodily reactions? In terms of firm belief? Attempts to answer these questions lead into a maze of further questions which are far removed from the spirit of the New Testament.

More will be said about the matter of legalism in chapter four. But it is important to recognise at this point that the importance of the conviction of sin in the beginning of the Christian life does not lie in its being a distinct and separable stage. Rather it is an *element* in conversion in the sense that it is part of what 'being converted' means. No one is converted whose experience does not include conviction of sin, for conversion registers the fact that a person has been turned from his old life of rebellion against God to a new life of commitment to Him. And it is inconceivable that such a change should take place without the person being convinced that he is a sinner.

But if conviction is one necessary element in conversion, if it gives part of the meaning of what it means to be converted, what are the other elements?

2: *Repentance without Faith*

The previous chapter was concerned with the fact that there is no conversion or effectual call by God without conviction of sin, though there may be conviction of sin without true conversion. But in saying that conviction of sin is necessary for conversion it is not to be supposed that the Bible teaches that a separate and separately identifiable period of conviction of sin is necessary. Rather, conviction of sin is one element or strand in conversion, without which conversion would be unintelligible. And to say that conviction of sin is one element or condition of conversion is not to say that it is a condition which a person may be supposed to have to fulfil, like one half of a bargain. Conviction of sin is not a condition which a person must achieve in order to qualify for divine grace. It is itself an effect of divine grace. To be a properly formed human being it is necessary to have a pair of lungs, but possessing a pair of lungs is not something which a human body can acquire for itself; it is part of what being a properly formed human body *is*. A person cannot convince himself of sin in order to merit or qualify for God's grace. Rather, being convinced of sin is one element in the complex experience of being converted, one without which there is no conversion because that is what conversion *is*.

The element of conviction of sin is necessary but it is not sufficient to constitute true conversion. What else, then, is necessary? In this chapter and the next an attempt will be made to answer this question.

It is helpful to reconsider the account of what happened on the Day of Pentecost (*Acts 2*). Those to whom Peter was preaching were 'pricked in their hearts'; their consciences troubled them. What happened next? They called out spontaneously to Peter and to the other apostles, 'Men and brethren, what shall we do?' Their conviction of sin was not stifled or suppressed as it was in the case of Felix and of the Rich Young Ruler. As they realised their guilt they expressed deep concern. But what is vital here is not that their response was public, a cry that everyone heard, or that it took the particular form that it did. A cry of penitence may be inaudible. It may be uttered in private. What matters is that in true conversion there is an expression of concern, of need. As was shown in the previous chapter, such a concern is due to the regenerating grace of God the Holy Spirit.

When the crowd called out, Peter replied: 'Repent, and be baptised every one of you in the name of Jesus Christ for the remission of sins, and ye shall receive the gift of the Holy Ghost' (*v. 38*). He then explained that God had promised deliverance to them and told them much more about the gospel and the way of salvation (*v. 40*). Among the crowd were three thousand who 'gladly received' Peter's word. That is, when they heard the call to repent they repented. They were baptised and added to the church. And this pattern is repeated throughout the Acts of the Apostles (*3:19, 17:30, 26:20*). And incidentally, in saying that when they repented they would receive the gift of the Holy Ghost, Peter was not at all implying that their repentance could be effected without the work of the Holy Spirit, as though there were certain conditions which had to be fulfilled prior to the giving of the Spirit. Repentance itself is a fruit of the Spirit's work (*Acts 11:18; 2 Tim. 2:25*), the gift of the risen and exalted Prince of Peace to His church (*Acts 5:31*). Thus Peter was really saying that

[47]

the gift of the Holy Spirit to the church, the effects of which they had been witnessing, would be theirs also once they were truly converted people.

The necessity for repentance in conversion is seen not only in the sequences of conversions in the Acts of the Apostles, but elsewhere throughout the Scripture, so frequently that where it is not explicitly mentioned its presence must be inferred. Thus the ministries of both John the Baptist and of Christ Himself are characterised by the call to repentance and belief in the gospel (*Matt. 3:2, Mark 1:15*). Christ describes the essence of His ministry as that of calling sinners to repentance (*Matt. 9:13*) and regards repentance as being wholly appropriate when men are faced with His own presence and teaching among them (*Matt. 12:41*). Repentance is so important that the New Testament sometimes uses the word 'repentance' where it might have been expected to use words for conversion or salvation (*Luke 15:7*).

The vital character of repentance in the teaching of Christ can perhaps best be brought out by Jesus' response to the report which was brought to Him about the Galileans slaughtered by Pilate (*Luke 13:1*). Those who told Him about this evidently thought, or were inclined to think, that those who died in this way were specially sinful. For only the notoriously sinful could have experienced the judgment of God in such a dramatic way. But Christ quickly corrects them: 'Except ye repent, ye shall all likewise perish', meaning not by this that his hearers were to perish in a similarly dramatic fashion if they did not repent, but that they would perish as certainly and finally as those whom Pilate slaughtered.

According to Christ, repentance is crucial. Without it, a person will perish, that is, endure eternal separation from God. If conviction of sin is a necessary element in conversion, then so is repentance.

How is repentance to be understood? It is clearly not the same as the conviction of sin, otherwise Peter would not have called upon his hearers on the Day of Pentecost to repent, because they were already convinced of their sin.

In trying to understand what Scripture means by repentance, there are two dangers to be avoided. Repentance must not be sentimentalised, thought of in exclusively emotional terms, in terms of sorrow or feelings of regret or remorse. For not every case of sorrow or of regret is a case of repentance. A man may be sorry that he is getting old or that circumstances stop him doing what he wants to do and this plainly has nothing to do with repentance. Simply to produce feelings of sorrow in people, perhaps as a result of religious or evangelistic pressure, is not to bring about repentance.

Repentance is not a vague feeling of sorrow, some general mood or disposition. It is, specifically, sorrow *for sin*. It involves a change of view about ourselves, a change of mind. The phrase 'a change of mind' can however suggest something rather trivial and shallow. Someone changes his mind when he decides to paint the house green and not white, or when he decides to spend his summer holidays in Scotland rather than in Spain. But in the case of repentance the change of mind in question is something much more deep-seated and settled than this. It is not a change of opinion about some relatively minor matter but a change of mind about the deepest issues in life, a person's own moral and spiritual ideals and standards, his relationship to God. This change of mind is a thorough-going reassessment. Whereas previously the individual has striven to please himself rather than to please God by keeping His law, the penitent, convinced of his own sinfulness and the fact that he both falls short of the divine

[49]

standards and transgresses them, repudiates his past life. He judges it by the standard of God's law, which he now, through the Spirit's enlightening, approves of and submits to. He turns away in grief and with a deep-seated sense of unworthiness from those standards which previously governed him.

This is how it was with Peter's hearers on the Day of Pentecost. As Peter preached and showed them the truth about Jesus, about what had happened to Him and their own wicked part in His death, they were not only convinced of the truth of what Peter said but, instead of covering up what they had done or attempting to explain it away, they recognised the truth for the horrible reality that it was and repudiated the deed. They detached themselves from it, they put it away.

Such a deep-seated change, whether it occurs in a few seconds or over many months or years, stirs deep emotions. Old bonds of affection and allegiance are broken and new ones are formed. Instead of being committed to a life of secularism or of careless indifference to God or of formal religiosity or of self-justifying moralism a person commits himself to God in penitence. But while such a change is accompanied by an emotional upheaval it is not *simply* an emotional upheaval.

The second danger to be avoided in properly understanding what repentance is, is to suppose that it is concerned only with particular sins. Particular sins coming to the attention of the individual are often one of the causes of repentance. This can be seen, again, in the case of the Jews on the Day of Pentecost. They were convinced that in the death of Christ they had acted with almost unbelievable wickedness. But while they were convinced of this particular sin and repented of it as Peter called them to repentance, it would be wrong to think of them as repudiating this sin and nothing else. The 'change of mind' in repentance is not a change of mind only about particular actions but a change of mind about any action or disposition where this can be shown to be not in accordance with the command of God. It is as these actions are identified by the word of God as failures to keep God's law that a person repents of them, changes his mind about them.

This illustrates yet again how in conversion word and Spirit combine together. It is as the Spirit enlightens the mind with respect to the law of God as this is revealed in nature (*Rom. 2:14*), but more especially as it is revealed in Scripture (*Rom. 3:2*) and gives the individual a new heart, that the individual is penitent with respect to those matters. So someone who is, for whatever reason, imperfectly informed about the law of God, about what God properly requires of His creatures by way of obedience, but who is penitent, will have an incomplete repentance. Suppose, for example, that while a person is aware that stealing is wrong he is unaware that bad time-keeping is a form of stealing. Such a person will see no reason to be penitent about his bad time-keeping. Or suppose that while he recognises that idolatry is a sin he does not appreciate that the visual representation of 'Jesus' breaks the second commandment, then he will not be penitent about such matters if he uses such pictures. But the stance of a true penitent in that position will be: 'I want to be convinced of whichever of my actions are sinful, and when I am convinced of the sinfulness of any action then I will repudiate that action'.

In considering the 'change of mind' which is at the heart of repentance it is necessary also to bear in mind not simply the extent or potential extent of true repentance – those actions covered by the whole law of God – but also the *intensive* or inward character of repentance. The penitent person recognises that God's law is concerned not simply with actions, important though they are, but also with motives or intentions, the end aimed at in performing the action. So Scripture teaches that it is possible to have two people perform the same action, with the same consequences, and yet to do this with totally different and even opposed moral and spiritual outlooks. In, say, refraining from stealing, the aim of the one may simply be to contribute to the good of society or to prosper in business. The aim of the other may be to glorify God, recognising that stealing is against God's law and that the law is concerned not only with the action of stealing but with covetousness, a state of heart or mind which may be present even when the opportunities for stealing do not occur.

It is the appreciation of the fact that penitence is both extensive – covering the whole of God's law – and intensive – having to do not only with action but also with motive and intention – that leads the penitent to use expressions which may otherwise seem extreme. The penitent, like Job, abhors himself (*Job 42:6*). Like David, he recognises that the Lord desires truth in the inward parts (*Ps. 51*). Like Isaiah, an awareness of the holiness of God makes him recognise that he is unclean (*Is. 6:5*). Such people are not only penitent over particular sins or over sin in general, they are penitent over *themselves*. Yet this must not be misunderstood. When Job abhorred himself this was not an expression of suicidal despair. Nor was Job attributing his sins to his body and wishing to be free of it. Rather, Job recognised the deep-seatedness of sin, its capacity to deceive him. In abhorring himself he wished in the strongest possible terms to be rid of that sinful self, the 'old man' as Paul put it, his old personality which he hated and which he condemned and yet which he could not, not even with the help of God's Spirit, gain complete victory over or free himself completely from in this life (*Rom.* 7).

So repentance reveals a moral and spiritual change, a change not merely in a person's moral stance, in moral behaviour or outlook, but a change which reaches into the innermost recesses of a person's spirit, to his thoughts, intentions and desires, as they are seen for what they are in the light of the word of God. Such a change can only properly be produced by the work of the Holy Spirit who grants repentance, the gift of the risen Christ to His people (*Acts 5:31*).

THE APPROPRIATENESS OF REPENTANCE

Why repentance? In the introduction to this study it was emphasised that Christian conversion signals the beginning, in the experience of the individual, of his being remade as a person. It is the start of the restoring in him of God's image, his re-forming as 'a new man', a member of the new humanity under the headship of the last Adam (*1 Cor. 15:45*). The work of procuring the redemption and restoration of sinners through Christ is God's work, undertaken at God's initiative. And the work of publishing and making known this good news is God's work, undertaken at His initiative, in the giving of divine revelation. Similarly the work of applying this saving work of Christ to the individual, of uniting him to Christ and enabling him to benefit from Christ's death and resurrection is God's work, undertaken at His initiative. Redemption in both its objective accomplishment and in its subjective application is God's work. And in this sense the work of conversion is wholly appropriate.

But there is a further sense in which penitence is wholly appropriate to God's purpose of remaking men and women in Christ. The basic relationship between God and His mankind is moral and spiritual. Man was created for the fellowship of God, a heart-to-heart relationship of mutual love and trust based upon God's law of love. This is a unique relationship. It is not to be compared to human friendships, however deep, for friendships are between equals and are informal in character. If such fellowship is to be restored through Christ it must involve the appropriate moral and spiritual change, not merely a change in moral status – the removal of guilt through the atonement of Christ – but also a change in personal relationship. Hence the promise, 'I will write my law in their hearts. . .' (*Jer. 31:33, Heb. 10:16*).

Conversion is thus necessary and is to be expected when God is at work graciously restoring the severed relationship between Himself and those who are created in His image. And repentance is a necessary element in this. It is unfortunate that often 'repentance' suggests something which is wholly negative and even harsh. It is thought of almost exclusively in terms of what is repented of. But the 'change of mind' which repentance signifies is not a mere emptying of the mind and it is certainly not a narrowing or closing of the mind. It is a renewing of the mind. B. B. Warfield says it is

> that fundamental change of mind by which the back is turned not upon one sin or some sins, but upon all sin, and the face definitely turned to God and to His service – of which therefore a transformed life is the outworking.

In understanding repentance emphasis should be placed equally upon the repudiation of the past life, the 'old man', and upon the positive approval and fostering of that which is good and holy. Repentance, true repentance, involves a turning from idols to serve the living and true God (*1 Thess. 1:9*).

How could a person reasonably or consistently expect to

enjoy close fellowship with God, the 'knowledge' of God, while still approving of his old way of life rooted in sinful attitudes and behaviour? He could only do so if he permitted himself the most blatant hypocrisy, a profession of love to God while still adhering to his old ways. His old preferences must be eradicated. This is the work of a life-time. But the decisive break and change is made at conversion when the old life is forsaken and there is delight in God's law (*Rom. 7:22*), the basis of renewed fellowship with God.

SORROW FOR SIN WITHOUT REPENTANCE

But as there can be conviction of sin without true repentance, so there can be sorrow for sin without true repentance. The Bible holds out this serious prospect, that a person's sorrow for sin may not be the fruit of true penitence but of something else. This can be seen from a number of biblical passages.

(1) *The rich young ruler again.* After Jesus had called on the young man to sell his property and to give the proceeds to the poor, he went away sorrowful (*Matt. 19:22*). Though Christ had bidden him to sell everything and to follow him, in fact the young man left Christ. His interest in the Saviour shrank to the point of vanishing the moment Christ identified his covetousness. And yet he was very sorrowful. What was this sorrow?

A person's sorrow can have various causes. In the case of the rich young ruler it seems that his sorrow was due to his realisation that he could not be both a follower of Christ and a covetous man. It was not sorrow for his covetousness and a repudiation of it because of its sinfulness, but sorrow at the realisation that he could not have both Christ and his love of money. It was the sorrow of tension rather than the sorrow of repudiation, the sorrow of a failure to achieve certain irreconcilable aims or ambitions. This kind of sorrow is frequently experienced. It is impossible to spend the same pound in two different ways. It is impossible to be in two places at the same time. The realisation of these facts often creates sorrow. But such sorrow has little to do with true penitence for sin. The rich young ruler realised as Jesus spoke to him that he could not have eternal life as long as he was covetous. He was very sorrowful when he realised this. But he remained covetous.

(2) *The Corinthian contrasts*. In the course of writing to the Corinthian church Paul draws two very illuminating contrasts:

> For though I made you sorry with a letter, I do not repent, though I did repent: for I perceive that the same epistle hath made you sorry, though it were but for a season. Now I rejoice, not that ye were made sorry, but that ye sorrowed to repentance: for ye were made sorry after a godly manner, that ye might receive damage by us in nothing. For godly sorrow worketh repentance to salvation not to be repented of: but the sorrow of the world worketh death. For behold this selfsame thing, that ye sorrowed after a godly sort, what carefulness it wrought in you, yea, what clearing of yourselves, yea, what indignation, yea, what fear, yea, what vehement desire, yea, what zeal, yea, what revenge! In all things ye have approved yourselves to be clear in this matter (*2 Cor. 7:8–11*).

Paul is writing here about one specific matter and he is writing to people who were already Christians. Nevertheless the contrast he draws between the feeling of regret and a complete change of mind is of more general interest. When the Apostle had previously written to the Corinthians they had been grieved by what they read and Paul had regretted this. But to Paul's joy the result of his letter had been that the Corinthians had repented of their conduct.

Then follows the remarkable analysis of godly sorrow and true repentance. Godly sorrow, Paul says, gives rise to true repentance, that repentance which consists in a deep-seated change of mind towards sin and which results in a changed life. Godly sorrow is to be contrasted with 'the sorrow of the world' (*v. 10*) which works death. So for Paul not all sorrow is the same. Godly sorrow issues in repentance and life while the sorrow of the world results in hardening and in death. And the repentance which godly sorrow results in is not mere regret but a radical change of outlook.

What, then, is the contrast? It is the contrast between sorrow at some loss or setback of a purely natural kind and sorrow at the realisation that one's conduct has been ungodly. There could be no greater contrast. If someone suffers a setback in his career or in his health or through the death of a friend or relation it is quite natural that there should be sorrow. The Bible does not condemn this. In some circumstances it condemns the absence of such sorrow (*Is. 57:1*).

But in saying that the sorrow of the world works death Paul had something else in mind. He rejoiced that his earlier letter sent to reprimand the Corinthians had met with genuine sorrow for sin. This was shown by their eagerness to make amends and by the absence of resentment or despair which would have had a spiritually hardening effect. This if unchecked would lead to spiritual death as it did for example in Pharaoh's case (*Ex. 9:27, 34*). By contrast godly sorrow is sorrow brought on by recognition of the fact that one has broken God's law and is unrighteous in God's sight, coupled with a desire to repudiate this way of life. As the term implies, godly sorrow arises from the recognition of one's failure in the sight of God, a sorrow which cannot be compensated for by any gain in earthly or material terms.

But the passage from 2 Corinthians is important and revealing in another respect. Not only does Paul draw the contrast between two sorts of sorrow, the godly sorrow which gives rise to repentance and life and the sorrow of the world which works death (*v. 10*), he also contrasts *repentance* and *regret* (*v. 8*). Paul regretted that the Corinthians had been grieved by the letter which he wrote to them, and which had led them to repentance, but he did not repent having sent it. Regret is not necessarily repentance. Paul's regret at the Corinthians' sorrow was not repentance for having caused it.

So there are two kinds of sorrow which must be distinguished from the godly sorrow which gives rise to and accompanies true repentance. There is the sorrow which results from the realisation of some loss or setback, sorrow which may result in hardening. And there is regret which may arise over the conduct of others, over something which was completely outside one's control, or over the particular consequences that one's action has had.

(3) *The repentance of Judas Iscariot (Matt. 27:3–5)*. Not only does the Scripture distinguish between two kinds of sorrow, godly sorrow and sorrow of the world, and between repentance and regret, it also distinguishes between two kinds of repentance.

Following Judas' betrayal of Jesus it became clear that the Jewish leaders were determined to put Jesus to death. When Judas realised this he 'repented himself, and brought again the thirty pieces of silver to the chief priests and elders, saying, I have sinned in that I have betrayed the innocent blood'. But this was not Judas' conversion.

Judas repented but he did not *truly* repent. What is the difference? It is not that Judas was sorry at being found out, because his act of betrayal was already publicly known. He was sorry at the outcome, not realising or not believing that his betrayal of Christ was to have this result. Judas' repentance was the repentance of despair, as his suicide shows. He regretted that his action had had the consequences which now he saw it having and it was perhaps this which led him to see the immorality of what he had done. He had a sense of justice, but he wanted to set matters right, not with God but only with those who had bribed him.

The example of Judas is a reminder that not all such repentance is cynical. There are, no doubt, cases of 'repentance' which are not due to the belief that what has been done is in any sense wrong, but the sorrow is due to the shame of being found out and the consequent inability to pursue the immorality further. So a convicted shop-lifter may express his sorrow to the judge, not because he is sorry for his shoplifting, for its illegality, but because his behaviour has been made public and further shoplifting made much more difficult.

But not all repentance is like this as Judas' case shows us. Judas recognised the immorality of his action. He had betrayed innocent blood and he knew it. It was this recognition that caused his repentance. And the penitence of many whose morality is totally secular, without any belief in God or in God as the source of moral authority, can be like this. Such persons may be genuinely sorry because of their moral failure. They have failed to keep certain standards which they believe it is proper for them to keep and they are sorry either because of the personal failure this reveals or because of the pain their action has brought upon others and upon themselves, or for both of these reasons. But this genuine sorrow is not penitence before God.

The regret of those who are deterred from immorality by the force of outward circumstances ought perhaps to be considered in a little more detail. The current debate about nuclear weapons has made the idea of *deterrence* a familiar one. The main justification for retaining such weapons is, it is claimed, to deter a potential aggressor, to frustrate his aggressive intentions by the belief that should he attack his action will have appalling consequences for himself and his allies. In similar terms the institution of punishment in the legal system is often justified in terms of the deterrent effect of the threat of punishment, or of actual cases of punishment, upon would-be offenders. Where punishment or the threat of it is sufficient to deter, as doubtless it is in some cases, then there are often feelings of regret. But this is the regret of someone who has been frustrated from doing what he wants to do, the regret of not achieving certain aims because of the interference of others. There is no regret at having had those aims in the first place. The would-be shoplifter who is deterred by the thought of a fine or of a prison-sentence if he is caught regrets not being able to steal. This is shown by the fact that if the restraint were lifted or if he believed that it was lifted, say during a period of the general breakdown of law, then he would gladly join the looters. In such cases there has been no change in basic outlook, only a change in behaviour brought on by the deterrent effect of punishment.

A COMMON FACTOR

The cases considered in the previous section are obviously not intended to be exhaustive. There are many more such cases, and real life is often more complex than their consideration suggests because elements from each can join together in one person's experience. It has been suggested that each of those which have been examined is an instance of some kind of penitence or sorrow or regret which is not true repentance in the sense in which Scripture regards repentance as being a necessary strand or element in conversion to Christ. Is it possible to say what each of these cases has in common?

It is hazardous to attempt this sort of enquiry, because of the diversity of cases. But what all these cases of 'repentance' or sorrow appear to have in common is that they occur in a context of self-justification. This framework may not be understood or expressed as such, but it is implied.

Part of this framework is a recognition of personal responsibility for keeping or flouting moral rules or standards however these are understood. Personal responsibility implies readiness to accept praise or blame as fair and to make no serious attempt to explain away all wrongdoing in terms of social or psychological factors, such as social class or upbringing. It is the belief in the co-presence of these two factors, the existence of moral standards and the recognition of personal responsibility, which accounts for the beliefs that people have that they have done wrong and the feelings of shame, sorrow and frustration which follow.

There is another crucial factor in this framework, besides the existence of moral standards and of belief in personal responsibility. It is the idea, often only vaguely realised and expressed but sometimes felt and expressed very acutely, that personal or social fulfilment – personal moral worth – lies in observing these moral rules or standards. This is so in the case of the biblical examples discussed earlier – where God's existence is explicitly presupposed – and it is also the case in the secular moralities of the present day. Whether expressed in religious terms or in secular, non-religious terms the attitude is the same. It is the belief that personal worth or goodness lies at least partly in keeping moral rules or standards, and the belief that often – perhaps more often than not – such standards are satisfactorily kept.

In the older literature sorrow at personal moral failure is often called 'legal repentance'. But this phrase, useful and accurate as it has been, rings a little oddly in the modern situation for a variety of reasons. For one thing the word 'legal' suggests to modern ears the law of the land, the legal system, and then it seems as if 'legal repentance' has something to do with sorrow on account of law-breaking in this sense. But this would be a serious misunderstanding. For the law of the land may or may not be moral. The word 'legal' in 'legal repentance' does not have to do with the legal system in England or in some other country, but with the spirit of the repentance, the *kind* of repentance that it is. More on this in due course.

A second reason why 'legal repentance' is misleading or inaccurate is that when it was used in the older literature it uniformly presupposed the belief that morality is a matter to do with God's law. This presupposition was realistic at the time but it is questionable whether it is realistic now when secular views of morality are so prevalent and when even in religious morality there is a reluctance to understand morality in terms of the will of God. Yet the frame of mind which has been, historically, characterised as 'legal penitence' is much more widespread than that phrase now suggests and it is certainly not confined to those who believe that morality has to do with the law of God.

What is this frame of mind? Presupposing some moral standard and some view of individual personal morality, it is the sorrow prompted by personal moral failure to keep to those standards which a person believes he can keep and which his moral worth or moral standing as an individual consists in keeping. Such sorrow may lead to an increased resolve to do better in future or it may lead to despair as it did with Judas, but in all cases the horizon of the individual is bounded by the idea that personal moral worth consists in keeping the rules. The sense of failure and frustration may be felt in a mild and intermittent way, or it may become deep and overwhelming, as it did, for example, in the cases of Martin Luther and John Bunyan. Bunyan wrote in his autobiography, *Grace Abounding to the Chief of Sinners*, that he

> fell to some outward reformation, both in my words and life, and did set the commandments before me for my way to heaven; which commandments I also did strive to keep, and, as I thought, did keep them pretty well sometimes, and then I should have comfort; yet now and then should break one, and so afflict my conscience; but then I should repent, and say I was sorry for it, and promise God to do better next time, and there get help again, for then I thought I pleased God as well as any man in England (*para. 30*).

What is significant about what Bunyan writes is that his repentance was followed by a renewed resolve 'to do better next time', in the belief that he could do better and could please God by doing better. He saw his failure as a setback but his basic belief in his own ability to please God remained intact. And even where, as in the case of Judas, repentance gives way to despair it is the despair of someone who, having lost all confidence in himself to please God, is not able to look to God for mercy.

This is the crucial difference between repentance which is mere sorrow for moral failure and that repentance which is an essential strand in the experience of true conversion. The difference lies in a different frame of mind. Whereas the 'legal' penitent thinks in terms of his own ability to please God the true penitent regards his moral failure as an offence against God and he repudiates it because it is an affront to the holiness and goodness of God. He gives up any hope of pleasing God by his own efforts. This is what Paul meant when he said, 'I was alive without the law once: but when the commandment came, sin revived, and I died' (*Rom.* 7:9). He here speaks of his *death*. Not the death of his body, of course, but when he came, through the work of God in his soul, to realise that the law of God reached to his heart, any hope of gaining acceptance with God through the law collapsed and he 'died'. The whole framework of his life underwent an enormous upheaval, a move from a situation in which his basic assumption was that he could please God to one in which he realised that he could not please God and needed rather to call upon God for mercy.

It is this shift in perspective, whether it comes gradually or suddenly, that people partly refer to when they say that the Christian faith begins to 'make sense'. Not that it was literally nonsense to them before, for they could understand the words and sentences that make up the Christian gospel, but they now under the Holy Spirit's enlightening come to believe that they themselves are precisely in that condition which the gospel is designed to meet.

This underlines one important matter that emerged earlier: in discussing the conviction of sin and now in discussing the nature of repentance, the focus of Scripture is not upon 'feelings'. Penitence or sorrow of whatever kind is not primarily a feeling. It is first and foremost a *belief* or a set of beliefs about God, about oneself, about the law of God, about one's moral failure and how one sees it, and so forth.

It may be that such beliefs and the feelings which accompany them are not perfectly understood by the person who has them. As one can make mistakes about others so one can make mistakes about oneself. And due to the influence of false ideas, perhaps in turn the result of false or distorted teaching about the Christian faith, it is perfectly possible for a person to misunderstand his own state. Such cases give rise to numerous pastoral problems and this is not the place to go into them. But they are one more reminder of the need to assess the spiritual state of other people with charity and restraint.

SUMMING UP

In the earlier part of this chapter it was shown that the Scripture teaches that repentance is a necessary strand in true conversion. It is not a condition to be fulfilled in order to be converted and much less is it to be thought of as a way of ingratiating oneself into the favour of God, but it is part of what being converted *means*. Those who are truly converted come to have certain beliefs about themselves and their relation to God and His law which leads them to a revulsion from their sins, a turning away from them on account of their sinfulness. But not everything which goes by the name of repentance is repentance in this sense. Those who are sorrowful because of their moral failure while still retaining a confidence in their own ability to please God by keeping His law do not experience, in such sorrow, true repentance. For they have not undergone the radical change of mind with respect to God's law, that recognition that they are unable to justify themselves by keeping the law, which is the hallmark of the penitence of a truly converted person.

3: *Faith and Repentance*

Christian conversion is composed of various elements or strands. These elements together tell us what conversion *is*. As has been seen, one of these strands is the conviction of sin, a person's recognition of his failure to keep the law of God, a recognition of personal accountability to God because of guilt. Yet it is possible to have such convictions and not to be converted. A further element in conversion is repentance, a turning from sin, a repudiation of personal lawlessness. But Scripture indicates that there are different kinds of repentance. There is the repentance which is regret at having one's purposes frustrated. There is repentance which is prompted merely by deterrence. It is possible for a person to be penitent and regretful as Judas was and yet not to be converted. For, while being filled with regret and remorse, a person can still in his deepest intentions adhere to his sinful views and keep up his sinful behaviour.

According to Scripture repentance is a change in mind, a change in a person's fundamental outlook in which his inner, deepest judgment about his own course of life is transformed from being opposed to God to being God-centred. It is a *decisive* change, brought about by the work of the Holy Spirit. Yet it is not a *complete* change in the sense that a true penitent is no longer attracted by his former life. He is still greatly attracted by it. But this is so in spite of himself. And so there arises the conflict between 'flesh' (the old, sinful self) and 'spirit' (the 'new man', the gift of the Holy Spirit), a conflict which will continue until death (*Rom.* 7).

How is the difference between true and false repentance to be understood and explained? It has already been stressed that true repentance comes about as a result of the working of the Holy Spirit in a person's mind and heart. True repentance is not the result merely of human decision or resolve, but it is God's gift of a new nature from which new decisions and resolves flow. And true repentance arises in the context of a person's trust in the mercy of God as this is revealed in Christ. True repentance and saving faith are the inseparable twin gifts of God the Holy Spirit, the Spirit of Christ, to an individual. Repentance arises *in the context of* saving faith. An attempt will now be made to be more precise about this.

WHAT IS FAITH?

According to Scripture, saving faith is a person's reliance upon God's mercy as revealed in Jesus Christ, and as displayed by Him on the cross. Such faith is central to biblical religion. It justifies the believer. It is the way in which the redemption obtained by Christ, by His life, death and resurrection – forgiveness and righteousness for sinners – is applied to the individual sinners for whom Christ died. Like true repentance this faith is the gift of God, one of those gifts purchased by Christ by His death and conveyed to individuals by the Holy Spirit. Whereas previously a person placed his confidence in himself, or in some person or authority other than God, or despaired of anyone and anything, now that person through the enlightening and strengthening work of the Spirit relies upon God for mercy. And in casting himself upon God's mercy in this way, in relying on another, what that other achieved on his behalf becomes his. It is reckoned to him. As W. G. T. Shedd put it

> Faith is wholly occupied with *another's* work, and *another's* merit. The believing soul deserts all its own doing, and betakes itself to what a third person has wrought for it, and in its stead.

There cannot be such faith without awareness of what God has done and so faith is reliance upon the word of God, what He has revealed of Himself. Saving faith, the faith which is the product of the Spirit in regeneration, is always informed by the word of God. Here is another important way in which in conversion the word of God and the Spirit of God are united together. Saving faith is not a blind leap. It is not a substitute for knowledge, as if faith begins to operate when knowledge peters out, as a person may still have confidence in an idea when there is no evidence for it. Nor is faith opposed to knowledge. It is reliance upon God's revelation, His actions, declarations and promises.

So there cannot be such faith without a knowledge of God's revelation. Such knowledge may be fragmentary and it may not be deep. It may be second-hand in the sense that it is derived by the person who has it not directly from the Bible or from Bible exposition but passed on by word of mouth. A believer may not even know that there is a Bible. But somehow or other he must come to know of the revealed mercy of God in Jesus Christ. Faith is reliance on that mercy.

It is sometimes said that true faith is not faith in the word of God but faith in *God*. But this contrast is based upon a misunderstanding. For if faith is taking God at His word then there is no opposition between God and the word of God. The word of God is God's speech, without which the character and intentions and promises of God would not be known. And in relying upon God's speech a person is relying upon God. If a person believes Christ's invitation, 'Come unto me . . . and I will give you rest' (*Matt. 11:28*) and as a result comes to Christ and gains rest, then in relying upon Christ's word he has relied upon Christ and in responding to Christ's invitation he has come to Christ.

Faith is faith in the word of God and such faith is faith in God Himself. What the believer believes in essence is that Christ is the Saviour of sinners and that whoever comes to Him will be saved, and the believer entrusts himself to Christ. Saving faith is not a person's belief that he has been saved by Christ nor even that Chirst has died for him in particular. It cannot be this because until he trusts in Christ in order to be saved he has no reason to think that Christ has died for him in particular or that Christ has saved him. For that person to believe that Christ has saved him before trusting Christ would be for him to believe something which is not true. In entrusting himself to Christ he is saved, and entrusting himself to Christ means casting himself upon His mercy. It is not believing that He has been merciful, but trusting Him for mercy. Faith is in order to receive mercy. It is not belief that one has received mercy.

Such faith justifies. But why is justification *by faith*? Is this an arbitrary matter? There is reason to think not, for there is a particular appropriateness about the connection between justification before God and faith. As has been seen faith expresses confidence in another, and not in oneself. And in relying upon another, upon Christ as Saviour and Lord, the believer makes it clear that he rejects any idea of self-reliance or self-merit in obtaining salvation (*Eph. 2:9*).

Saving faith, accompanied by and arising out of the conviction of sin, is inseparably accompanied by true repentance. Together they form the three essential strands to true Christian conversion. So it is appropriate that an attempt be made to say more about what true repentance is.

TRUE REPENTANCE – SOME EXAMPLES

As in previous chapters it is helpful to look at actual biblical examples in order to formulate the idea of true repentance more clearly.

(1) *The Pharisee and the publican* (*Luke 18:9–14*). In telling this parable Jesus was prompted by the attitude of those who were self-confident about their 'righteousness', their moral standing in God's sight, and who as a consequence were proud and despised other people (*v. 9*). Like many of Jesus' sayings, this parable was designed to shock His hearers by overturning their preconceptions and established ways of thinking. What is shocking here is that the Pharisee who had a reputation for religion is treated by Jesus in the parable as being basically irreligious while the publican who was a social outcast is shown to be justified in God's sight (*v. 14*).

The Pharisee was self-assured in God's presence. His thanks to God seem superfluous. The publican, by contrast, had a clear awareness of his own unworthiness before God. He stood far off from God's presence (*v. 13*). Repentance has to do with a person's relationship with God. Although the Pharisee prayed to God, his thoughts were centred upon himself, and upon his relationship with other people. He was, he thought, 'not as other men are', and certainly not like the publican (*v. 11*). But the publican's all-consuming concern was with God. He hardly dared to approach God because he recognised God's holiness and majesty and his own sinfulness. He believed that he was not fitted to come to God. And he expressed deep sorrow for his sin. He smote upon his breast. He made no excuses, much less did he assume a basic self-righteousness. He recognised his own responsibility to God.

It is most important for understanding true repentance to see that the penitent publican called upon God for mercy. He saw his need of mercy. He did not presume that he had it or that he was entitled to it. But he knew that God *was* merciful. In the last chapter the connection between one kind of repentance and utter despair was noted. But the publican's penitence was not of this kind. He prayed in the Temple, God's house, the visible token of God's presence with His people Israel, the God who revealed Himself to Moses as a God of mercy (*Ex. 34:6*) and whose mercies were the continued experience of Israel (*Ps. 89:1*).

The publican realised that relief for his condition could only come at the behest of God in not exercising judgment – which he deserved, and which would result in his condemnation – but rather in granting mercy which was undeserved and the result of which would be his forgiveness and his gracious acceptance by God. The true penitent despairs of himself but he does not despair of God. And the mercy of God is not something which the penitent presumes upon, but he comes to God at God's own initiative and invitation. The publican though aware that God is a God of mercy does not presume that God's mercy is his. He does not say 'Thank you for being merciful to me'. Rather, he *calls* for mercy: 'God be merciful to me a sinner'. Had he, before he called for mercy, been assured of God's mercy to him then there would have been no need for him to call out. His request would have been unnecessary, for there would have been nothing to ask for.

The publican's sorrow does not drive him away from God but to God. His conviction of sin is not an isolated experience, a cause of despair, but it is accompanied by confession to God. And yet the confession is implied rather than explicit. Unlike the Pharisee, the publican does not say very much. Why was this? Because he knew that God knew him. His repentance, in essence, consisted in knowing himself as God in His holiness knew him, and in putting his hope in God's mercy.

So the publican's cry of confession was not a cry of despair but of faith and of hope. It was prompted by the Spirit and founded on the revealed word of God.

In a sense 'God' is just a word. And in the pluralistic societies of the West there are numerous conceptions of God. Some are the result of human speculation and wishful thinking, while some are based on the influence of religions other than Christianity, and others are based upon Christianity and distortions of Christianity. If a person comes to God it is vital to ask, to *which* God is the person coming? Conversion is the joint product of the work of the Spirit of the true God and the word of the true God. But if, due to his ignorance or to factors beyond his control such as the general cultural climate in which he lives, a person's idea of God is unbalanced or distorted then the character of that person's conversion will be similarly distorted. It is therefore important that everyone gains the fullest and the most accurate knowledge of God, the true God, from what He has revealed of Himself through Scripture and supremely in the Scriptural record of Christ. The desire for such increased and accurate knowledge is itself the result of the guidance and prompting of the Spirit.

The example of the publican shows that true repentance is inseparable from faith in God and in Christ. This may seem surprising for it may appear that repenting and believing are distinct acts and that 'repentance' and 'faith' mark distinct phases of experience: the grief of penitence is followed by the joy of saving faith. Some experiences of conversion may be like this. But other experiences may be different. There is a danger that an idea of conversion will be gained solely from human experience, even from one person's experience. But the Holy Spirit in conversion works variously in different people, and the understanding of conversion is to be gained, not from such varieties of experience, but from the word of God.

(2) *The Corinthian contrasts again (2 Cor. 7)*. Attention has already been given to the contrasts which Paul drew between regret and repentance, and between godly repentance and 'the sorrow of the world'. Paul goes on, particularly in verse 11, to show in detail what the nature of this godly sorrow is.

Penitence is not a feature only of a person's conversion. The Christian life is a life of continuing penitence, for the Christian is continuously made aware of his remaining sin, of the wickedness of his own heart, and of how far short he falls of the divine standards. Conversion is not some past event or crisis which grows dimmer and the effect of which becomes weaker as the years pass. Rather, if a person has been converted then as far as the New Testament is concerned he is now converted. And if he is now converted then he has been converted. And although there may be periods of darkness when a person is able to gain comfort from remembering God's past goodness (*Num. 14:11–20*), and certainly God's past mercies should never be forgotten (*Ps. 103:2*), nevertheless present experience is the crucial test of the genuineness of the past experience. For if a person is not now converted he has never been converted.

The situation in 2 Corinthians is one in which Paul calls the church to penitence because of a particular sin and rejoices that his letter has moved them to godly sorrow which worked repentance to salvation (*v. 10*). The sign that their repentance was true repentance is given by Paul in the following verse. Faced with their own responsibility for sin the Corinthians had been roused from apathy. They became indignant with themselves over their previous laxity. They came to have fresh respect for Paul's apostolic authority and a renewed desire to see Paul again, to support him, and to see justice done in the church.

Repentance is active. It is not inert and passive, a fatalistic self-pity. It is the rousing of the self actively to repudiate the former life. It is a turning from the old course of life but it does not simply imply a cessation of evil, the gaining of a position of neutrality. In repudiating the old life the new standards, the standards of God's law, are vigorously adhered to.

The two examples glanced at show a two-fold linkage between repentance and other things. In the first place repentance is inseparable from faith. Repentance is not unbelieving despair but it leads to hope in the mercy of God. In turning from the old life the individual turns – or rather, is turned – to God. In the second linkage repentance is active in repudiating the old life, in behaving in a way consistent with penitence. So repentance heralds the deepest possible moral change.

REPENTANCE IS INSEPARABLE FROM FAITH

This connection can be seen in the way in which the two are frequently joined together in the ministry of Christ and of the apostles. People are never called upon merely to repent but to repent and be baptised (*Acts 2:38*), to repent and believe the gospel (*Mk. 1:15*), to repent and be converted (*Acts 3:19*), to repent because the kingdom of God is at hand (*Matt. 4:17*). They come together in Christian experience (*1 Thess. 1:9*), even though sometimes 'repentance' is used in a wider sense which seems to encompass faith.

The two are linked together by the word of God. This comes first as a demand from God which a person through the enlightening work of the Holy Spirit realises that he is unable to fulfil, and then as gospel promise, the promise of mercy in Jesus Christ, the promised remedy for those who recognise their own failure. It is as the word of God is preached, as both demand and promise, that the Holy Spirit is pleased to work in renewing the minds and hearts of men and in bringing them to repentance and saving faith in Christ. If the promises of the gospel alone were proclaimed, then they would be unintelligible or beside the point to those to whom they are addressed. If the demand of God alone is preached without the prospect or well-grounded hope of mercy, then all that would result is despair as a person faces his moral failure with no expectation of relief or deliverance.

But the connection between the two is even closer. True repentance, the repentance which is the basic repudiation of sin, *follows* faith though it is not *caused by* faith. Being convinced of his sin a person may under the blessing of the Holy Spirit find his salvation from sin in Jesus Christ. And penitence and amendment of life flow from this reliance upon the Holy One of God. For how can Christ be relied upon for salvation if unholiness is not repudiated and if obedience to Him is not striven for?

Mistakes in understanding may arise here because sometimes repentance is confused with the conviction of sin. But there is an enormous difference between an awareness of sin and guilt before God, and a turning to God in penitence. A further possible source of misunderstanding lies in thinking of repentance in exclusively negative terms, in terms of the repudiation of and denial of the old sinful self. This is a part of repentance, but only a part, for repentance is concerned not only with the turning of the self away from sin but also with the desire to devote oneself to God. It is a moral change of the deepest kind. This is why Calvin, for example, defines repentance in very positive terms. It is

> the true turning of our life to God, a turning that arises from a pure and earnest fear of him; and it consists in the mortification of our flesh and of the old man, and in the vivification of the Spirit.

So repentance, the deep resolve to have done with sin and to live to God, is not a preliminary to faith – this would be to confuse it with the conviction of sin – rather it is the consequence of faith. In Christ's parable of the publican and the Pharisee the publican's contrition, his sense of unworthiness, is the outcome of his awareness that God is merciful, just as the godly repentance of the Corinthian church was due to their recognising the words of Paul to them in a letter as the authoritative words of an apostle of Jesus Christ.

The inseparability of repentance and faith in the way described is a proof of how mistaken it is to suppose that a person may 'take Jesus as Saviour' but not 'take Jesus as Lord'. This is incongruous because it supposes that it is possible to separate Christ in His work as Saviour from His moral and spiritual Lordship. But more to the point, it is incongruous because it supposes faith without repentance, faith in Christ without the desire or resolve for moral change arising from that faith. It supposes that a person might receive pardon from Christ for his sins without personally repudiating those sins and coming to have the desire to please God by a life of obedience to Him.

BUT REPENTANCE IS NOT FAITH

Repentance and faith are inseparable but this does not mean that they are indistinguishable. Repentance is accompanied by faith but repentance is not faith. They are not two ways of looking at the same thing. Repentance and faith are inseparable in experience but distinguishable in thought.

It is important to insist upon this in order to safeguard the purity of the biblical teaching regarding justification by faith alone. Scripture does not teach that justification is by repentance but by faith (*Rom. 4:24, 5:1*). When a person relies upon Christ for salvation then God freely forgives his sins for Christ's sake and imputes to him the perfect, personal righteousness of Christ (*Rom. 4:24*). His status before God is as if he had never sinned, and he has the righteousness of Christ reckoned to him. Personal justification occurs when a person relies upon the finished work of Christ and on that alone.

Why has God ordained that justification should be by *faith* and not by love or through repentance or in some other way? Is such an arrangement a completely arbitrary affair due simply to the 'whim' of God? It would be too hasty to conclude that it is. There is a special appropriateness about faith as regards justification. Faith is the beggar's hand which accepts the riches of Christ. Faith relies upon the work of Christ, trusting what He has done and not upon what the believer has done or may do. It is faith's reliant, out-going, confiding quality which makes it appropriate as the instrument of justification. Paul says, 'It (receiving God's righteousness) is of faith that it might be by grace' (*Rom. 4:16*). In order that salvation might clearly be, and be seen to be, by God's grace He has ordained that the blessings of salvation should be appropriated by faith – the outgoing, confiding, resting of the soul upon Christ.

To suppose that justification were by repentance would have two calamitous consequences. In the first place, the biblical teaching of salvation by divine grace alone would be radically compromised and undermined. For salvation by divine grace and salvation by works are utterly at odds. If salvation is by grace it cannot be by works, and *vice versa* (*Eph.* 2:8,9). And if justification were by repentance, and repentance is, as has been seen, the repudiation of the old life and the Spirit-given desire for the service and obedience of God, then justification could be no more by grace. It would be justification by works since repentance is a work, but true justification is by faith. Furthermore if justification were by repentance then the assurance of salvation would be an impossibility since repentance is a striving after obedience, and is necessarily imperfect and incomplete. A person would never be assured that his repentance was sufficient. So he would never be assured that he had appropriated God's salvation and could never be assured that he himself was personally saved.

So while faith and repentance are inseparable it is faith that saves because faith ensures an utter reliance upon Christ.

WHICH COMES FIRST?

Repentance is not and cannot be faith and hence justification is not by repentance but by faith. But which comes first, repentance or faith?

This question has given rise to a good deal of confusion and, in trying to get clear about it, it is necessary to draw some distinctions. In the first place it is important to distinguish between the *logical* order of faith and repentance (what older writers call 'the order of nature') and the sequence in time of faith and repentance ('the order of time'). Is repentance logically prior to faith, or *vice versa*? This is a question about whether an understanding of repentance depends upon a prior understanding of faith, or *vice versa*. And as was shown when discussing the relationship between repentance and faith, repentance is

to be understood in terms of faith. Repentance makes
sense in the light of what faith is. It is not faith that makes
sense because of what repentance is.

But to say that faith is conceptually or logically prior to
repentance tells nothing one way or the other about the
order of faith and repentance in Christian experience. To
suppose that faith is logically before repentance is not to
suppose that faith is prior to repentance *in time*, that there
is a time in a person's experience when he believes but
does not repent. In fact it has been seen that repentance is
the inseparable accompaniment of faith so that whoever
believes at the same time repents and whoever repents at
the same time believes. And this is not because the one
causes the other but because both are jointly the products
of the work of the Holy Spirit and the word of God. In
John Murray's words,

> There is no priority. The faith that is unto salvation is a
> penitent faith and the repentance that is unto life is a
> believing repentance.

But then there is the question of the relationship of faith
and repentance in self-conscious experience, the *felt*
awareness. And here both Scripture and experience
encourage the thought that there are great differences
between the experiences of different individuals. Some
people are aware of their repentance in a more dominant
way than they are of their faith while in the case of others
faith is more dominant and repentance muted. In the case
of some their experience seems to reveal that repentance is
prior to faith, while in the experience of others faith seems
to be prior to repentance. It is important to appreciate
such diversity for it prevents the church from thinking of
only one pattern of experience as 'orthodox'. It would be
most unwise to formulate the doctrine of conversion from
an inductive investigation of such experiences. Rather the

doctrine of conversion, as all Christian doctrines, should be derived from the Scriptures and Christian experience should be interpreted by Scripture.

When considering and describing religious experience (or indeed a person's experience of anything), it is important to distinguish between awareness and self-awareness. This can be illustrated from the conviction of sin. Earlier it was shown that conviction of sin is a necessary strand in the character of true Christian conversion. Without such conviction there is no true conversion. But it does not follow from this that a person must *be aware that* he is convinced of his sin in order for him truly to be convinced of sin, any more than he needs to be aware that he is seeing the only natural satellite of the earth in order to be seeing the moon. He may be aware not so much of his sins as of resting on Christ for salvation. Another person's experience of the conviction of sin and of penitence for sin may be so deep, lasting and distracting that he cannot fail to be aware of it. And he may be so preoccupied with his sins that he is unaware or unsure that he is also trusting Christ for his salvation when it is evident to others by his speech and behaviour that he is in fact doing so. Not only does Christian experience vary enormously between individuals but the level and degrees of self-awareness vary as well. So it is inadvisable to construct the doctrine of conversion (or of any other Christian doctrine) from evidence gained from what people say about their own felt experience. The elements of the doctrine of conversion must be drawn from Scripture, and this doctrine must be allowed to interpret and modify our experience.

SUMMARY

There are three strands to true Christian conversion. There is the conviction of sin. A person in being converted is convinced that before God he is guilty. He has broken God's law, and has no hope of keeping it. He recognises his own bondage to sin. A second strand is saving faith in Christ, the faith which justifies the sinner before God. Being convinced of his sin the sinner casts himself upon God's mercy. Such saving faith is accompanied by true repentance, the third strand in conversion. This repentance is a profound moral change. It is not simply the regret or remorse which accompanies a moral failure or setback nor is it the remorse of despair or the sorrow at being found out or deterred from sin. It is the godly sorrow which produces a profound revulsion against sin and a resolve to serve God and to delight in Him. All these changes in a person, the bringing about of conviction of sin, saving faith and true repentance, are the results of the regenerating work of the Holy Spirit. They are not produced by self-effort or by moral reform. The moral and spiritual energy required is imparted by God the Holy Spirit in granting spiritual awareness and strength of purpose as He renews the dead soul and sets about restoring the image of God in man.

There is need for caution at two levels. There is a great variety of experience of conversion. For some it is sudden, traumatic. For others it is gentle and almost imperceptible. Some are converted out of paganism or secularism in one sudden movement. Others are gradually converted, perhaps from a Christian or semi-Christian background. There is no stereotype or ideal or 'classic' conversion. The second ground for caution lies in the fact that, even granted such variety, there is scope for even greater variety and for self-misunderstanding at the personal level. This is because one person is not always aware to the same degree as another person of the presence of one or other of these various elements in his experience. It is advisable therefore to get clear on the essentials of conversion, not from gathering together and sorting through a multitude of personal accounts of spiritual experience but from Scripture. But by the same token the presence of such variety argues for caution and restraint in assessing the spiritual state of people, whether one's own or that of others. It is essential to adhere to Scriptural rules and standards.

Conversion is the beginning in the experience of the individual of the process of his being remade as a person. It is a profound moral and spiritual change which cannot be understood except by a framework of beliefs about God, His law, His grace in Christ and the needs of the human soul. More particularly such conversion is the hallmark of a characteristic piety or spirituality, which should be reflected in the family, in the church, and in society at large. Before we explore some elements of this spirituality, it may help to clarify matters further by considering certain difficulties and misconceptions which may arise from what has already been discussed.

4: *Problems*

Having considered the various elements or strands which together comprise Christian conversion, the beginnings of spiritual life in an individual, we shall in this chapter take up certain objections and difficulties some of which have already been noticed and postponed. Looking at these objections should help to clarify the beginnings of Christian life further.

'LEGALISM'

The term 'legalism' is often flung about as a general term of religious abuse but its meaning is almost always left unclear by those who use it. Some may be tempted to say that the claim that there are essential elements which together comprise true Christian conversion is 'legalistic'. Surely, it might be said, conversion is the work of God's free Spirit. To think of *essential* elements or conditions of conversion cuts across or goes against God's free grace in the gospel. For grace makes no demands and lays down no conditions. The central glorious fact of the Christian gospel is that God accepts sinners. Why be sidetracked from this by going into detail about the various requirements for true Christian conversion? Is this not going back to the very thing that the biblical gospel is designed to rid people of for ever – a preoccupation with and a reliance upon their own doings?

What is a legalist? One kind of legalist is the person who tries to gain God's favour or acceptance by keeping the law –

typically either the moral law or the ceremonial law or certain divine commands regarding the Christian ordinances of baptism and the Lord's Supper, or other rules which are mistakenly thought to have been commanded by God. A legalist insists on keeping this or that law or all laws in order to be justified, to gain acceptance with God. This can be termed *legalism in justification*. It was because they were legalists in this sense that Paul opposed the Judaisers in Galatia (*Gal. 2:16–21*).

Another kind of legalist is the person who insists that proper Christian discipleship requires the keeping of certain rules or principles which are not commanded by God in Scripture but which are either left open by God or which are forbidden. Suppose that someone insists that proper Christian behaviour requires one to be a vegetarian or to refuse to pay taxes. Vegetarianism is a practice which the New Testament leaves open. If a person wishes to be a vegetarian there is nothing in the New Testament to prevent him from being one, but also nothing which requires anyone to be a vegetarian. And so to insist upon vegetarianism, to regard meat-eating as sinful, is to contradict the teaching of the New Testament. Such an insistence would be legalistic. In a similar way if someone says that true discipleship requires the Christian to refuse to pay taxes (perhaps because Christ said that His kingdom was 'not of this world') this would be to reject a practice which the New Testament directly commands. The New Testament does not leave the payment or non-payment of taxes an open, indifferent matter, something which a person may choose or not, as it does the practice of vegetarianism. Rather it positively commands the Christian to pay his taxes. So to require Christians to refuse to pay taxes as part of their Christian profession would be to require something which is forbidden by Scripture. Either way, requiring something which is indifferent or requiring something which is forbidden, is legalistic. It is making laws where the New Testament makes no law. This may be called *legalism in sanctification*. It was because of the danger of legalism in sanctification that Paul wrote about 'things indifferent' and the 'weaker brother' in Romans 14.

Can it be said that in setting out the various essential strands or elements in Christian conversion, conditions for personal justification have been demanded which the New Testament does not require – that a subtle form of justification by works has been defended? Or can it fairly be alleged that, in saying that a person cannot be a true Christian unless he is convinced of his sin, believes and repents, conditions have been laid down which a person must fulfil before he can be a Christian? Where does the New Testament say that it is necessary to experience conviction of sin in order properly to be a Christian? Is not such an insistence a case of legalism in justification?

These worries are based upon a number of misunderstandings. It has been seen that justification is by faith alone. Any person is accepted by God who relies upon Christ alone for his salvation. To stress that justifying faith is accompanied by the conviction of sin and by evangelical repentance is not to promote these to the status of meritorious works. Rather, it is to fill out in a little more detail what justifying faith *is*. It is that faith which arises from the conviction of sin and is accompanied by sincere repentance. Suppose that in order to qualify for inclusion in the Olympics as a runner a person must achieve a certain time in the Olympic trials. Suppose as well that no one can achieve that time except those who train and that everyone who achieves this time has in fact well-developed leg-muscles. It would be foolish to say that (under these circumstances) there is not one condition for inclusion in the Olympics – achieving a certain time – but three conditions – achieving a certain time, training, and having well-developed leg-muscles. There is one condition – meeting the qualifying time – but that one condition is accompanied by other factors. Similarly with justification by faith alone. The doctrine of Christian conversion does not compromise the basic theological and spiritual principle that justification is by faith alone. But the faith which alone justifies is in fact accompanied by the conviction of sin and repentance.

What about legalism in sanctification? In setting out the doctrine of conversion is there not a danger of laying down conditions for Christian discipleship that the New Testament does not lay down? But why should there be this danger? What is conviction of sin? It is a person's belief that he himself is guilty before God in virtue of having failed to keep His law. How does having this belief compromise the nature of sanctification by making it legalistic? What commands are added to the divine commands by insisting upon the need for the conviction of sin? None at all! Rather the conviction of sin is only genuine conviction when it is based upon a proper understanding of God's law. Someone who believes that God justly threatens him with judgment for not being a vegetarian is not experiencing true conviction of sin. Such a person needs to become aware of the true content of the law of God.

What is repentance? Repentance is a sincere turning from sin to God. To know what true repentance is, not only does one need to have some awareness about what God forbids and hence what one is to turn from, but also what God commands and hence what one is to turn to. Such knowledge is necessary both to define the true nature of this repentance and to experience it. If someone thinks that turning from sin involves turning from meat-eating and turning to God in repentance involves vegetarianism such attitudes do not constitute evangelical repentance but need to be reformed by the knowledge of what God actually does forbid and require.

STRANDS NOT STAGES

It was precisely in order to avoid giving substance to the charge of legalism that it was stressed, in formulating the nature of Christian conversion, that conviction of sin, saving faith and repentance constitute not stages of Christian experience but *strands*, or *elements*. Why is this important, and why does talk of strands make a difference? Suppose the alternative and see how unsatisfactory it is. Suppose it was insisted that true Christian conversion is made up of a certain sequence of spiritual experience, say conviction of sin, followed by repentance, followed by saving faith. Or conviction of sin, followed by saving faith, followed by repentance. One would then be insisting not merely that certain elements must be present for there to be true Christian conversion, but that these elements must be formed into a certain pattern or sequence.

This would be legalistic. For while Scripture insists on the various elements which have been examined, nowhere does Scripture teach that these elements must form a certain pattern. So to insist on such a pattern would be legalistic for it would require something that Scripture does not require. And it is clear why Scripture does not require it. For suppose it did require a certain period of conviction of sin followed by a certain period of repent- ance followed by faith. A person who was concerned about his salvation and who was presented with such teaching, would at once take his eyes off Christ as the healer of his wounds and begin to be concerned as to whether or not he had properly fulfilled the conditions. And this would be fatal – it would be unevangelical and legalistic. For instead of being freed to flee to Christ a person is brought into

[87]

bondage to the fulfilling of certain conditions in his experience. It is surely for similar reasons to these that the Scripture does not insist that the experience of conviction of sin should be of a certain duration, say a week or a month, or of a certain measurable intensity. Thus Calvin says

> Lacking any semblance of reason is the madness of those who, that they may begin from repentance, prescribe to their new converts certain days during which they must practise penance, and when these at length are over, admit them into communion of the grace of the gospel.

And Leighton:

> There is an unspeakable lustre and beauty of the new creature, by the mixture of all the Divine graces, each setting off another, as so many rich several colours in embroidery; but who can trace that Invisible Hand that works it, so as to determine of the order, and to say which was first, which second, and so on; whether faith, or repentance, and all graces etc.? This is certain, that these and all graces do inseparably make up the same work, and are all in the new formation of every soul that is born again.

Finally, to talk of conversion in terms of strands rather than stages has the advantage of making clear that these strands are conditions in the logical rather than the causal sense. They are not conditions which have to be fulfilled in order for a person to be converted; rather they are what being converted *means*. Someone who approaches the question of conversion as though it were a matter of what he must do in order to be converted has completely misunderstood what conversion is. Such an approach suggests that the person is proceeding from the assumption that he has the power to fulfil these conditions. But it is not so much a matter of conditions being fulfilled by a person as changes being brought about in a person by the Holy Spirit and these changes having the multi-stranded character that has been discussed. Anyone changed in these ways is converted, for that is what conversion *is*. If someone were to say that marriage is hedged about with all sorts of difficult conditions – it is necessary for the bridegroom to love the bride, not to be already married, to have the ceremony validly performed, and so on – their comments would show a gross misunderstanding. Anyone who approached the matter of marriage thinking that these were burdensome conditions to be fulfilled and that there could be a marriage without any of these conditions would reveal that he does not know what marriage *is*. These are not to be thought of as conditions which anyone who wants to be married must fulfil. They are what marriage *is*. Similarly the strands of conviction, faith and repentance are not conditions which a person must fulfil and which, when he has achieved them, certify that he is converted. Rather together they are what conversion is, and those who are converted manifest, to a degree, each of these strands.

FAITH, ASSURANCE AND THE OFFER OF THE GOSPEL

It was seen earlier that saving faith is not a person's belief that he is already saved, nor is it a person's conviction that Christ has died to save *him*. Rather faith is the actual act of reliance upon Christ in order to be saved. The reason for this is clear. If God assured men in Scripture that everyone without exception was saved through Christ, or if He had provided in Scripture a directory of the names of all and only those who are saved through Christ, then perhaps a person would be entitled or warranted to believe, straight off, that Christ had died for *him*. Faith would then be accepting that when God said that all without exception were saved He was to be relied upon, or that when He published the directory of the names of the saved He was accurate, with no omissions and unwarranted additions.

But Scripture does not have that character. It does not say 'Christ died for all the world in such a sense that all the world will finally be saved'. The new humanity does not comprise everyone. Nor does Scripture contain a list of all the saved by name. Rather it provides a general offer or invitation to all without exception to come to Christ for salvation, as in *Matthew 11:28*: 'Come unto me, all ye that labour and are heavy laden, and I will give you rest', and *John 6:37*: 'Him that cometh to me I will in no wise cast out'. And it gives a general description of those who do come to Christ (the weary, the lost, the heavy-laden), of what it means to come to Christ (conviction of sin, faith, repentance), and of what it means to be in Christ (love to God and fellow Christians, joy, struggle with sin, desire to please God, and so on).

So faith, reliance upon Christ, is a response to the invitations of Christ in Scripture. A person relies *on Christ* for salvation. And that person's knowledge that he is converted, his assurance that he is God's child can only follow the initial act of faith as he is made aware that he is accepted by God and that he has the character of a true Christian. And so faith, which is trusting in Christ, and the assurance of faith, which is the confidence that a person has that he is accepted by God, are distinct things which ought never to be confused.

It is sometimes said that assurance is a reflex act of faith. This makes it clear that faith is distinct from assurance, but the terminology can be misleading. The word 'reflex' suggests something mechanical and automatic, like a knee-jerk or blinking, but there is nothing mechanical or automatic about a person becoming assured that he is a

Christian. Many have laboured with doubts about their personal acceptance with God for long periods. And assurance is gained when it comes not by some mechanical process but as a gift of God given through a person's reflection upon the work of God in his soul. This is what the old-fashioned terminology of 'reflex' was designed to capture, of course, the idea that assurance is in its very nature *reflective* upon faith.

A further possibly misleading connotation of the word 'reflex' is the implication that faith in Christ and assurance are always two distinct events or states, that first a person trusts Christ and only after that is he assured that he is Christ's. But there is no biblical warrant for such a view. This is another area besides that discussed in the previous chapter where it is important not to impose a pattern of experience which has no basis in Scripture. To maintain that, because faith and assurance are distinct ideas, therefore every believer must go through a period of faith without assurance and then at a later date be given assurance, is to adopt a view which is without warrant in Scripture.

In saying that faith and assurance are distinct the nature of saving faith is safeguarded, but the distinctness in question is a logical or conceptual distinctness. Because of what faith is it cannot be identified with assurance. But in some cases at least when God grants faith to an individual he also at the same time and in a way that is indistinguishable in that person's experience grants him assurance. Such a person may, the moment he believes, gain assurance that he is accepted with God. As far as his conscious experience is concerned, the two, faith and the assurance of faith, will be indistinguishable. Yet for all this they are distinct ideas and it is necessary to insist upon their distinctness in order that the character of true saving faith – as the reliance upon Christ for salvation – may properly be understood and protected. Once again, as with other areas to do with conversion, an individual's experience of God's saving grace must not be made the norm for the pattern of anyone else's experience, nor must the doctrine of saving faith be constructed out of experience however saintly. The doctrine of saving faith and assurance, as the doctrine of Christian conversion as a whole, must be derived from God's revelation about these things in Scripture.

A properly constructed train consists of an engine and carriages and wherever the engine goes the carriages go as well. Yet it would be unwise to conclude from the fact that the carriages go where the engine goes that there is no distinction between the carriages and the engine, that the engine *is* the carriages. It would be equally unwise to conclude that because the carriages normally go where the engine goes that there are never situations in which they become detached. So it is with faith and assurance. Faith and assurance normally go together. But this does not mean that faith *is* assurance. Faith may on occasion become detached from assurance and exist even in periods of spiritual doubt and darkness, and assurance may be detached from saving faith. This is the tragic condition of someone who has *false* assurance.

So assurance is logically secondary to saving faith and assurance is sometimes gained and typically retained by the believer by his becoming aware of the marks of God's grace in his own life and experience. The believer pays attention to the biblical injunction to make his calling and election sure (*2 Pet. 1:10*) and he tests himself by the 'tests of life' such as love to God (*1 Jn. 5:2*), love to the brethren (*1 Jn. 3:18*), the experience of peace with God (*Rom. 5:1*) and the presence of spiritual warfare (*Rom. 7*). Examining himself in this way he may come to gain assurance that he is a Christian or to retain the assurance that he already has.

Such examination is not a dispassionate or mechanical affair. As spiritual discernment is needed properly to understand and appropriate the teaching of God in Scripture, or His work in providence, so a person's discernment that he is in a state of grace, his appreciation of the evidence of the work of the Spirit in his life, is aided by the Holy Spirit. This is not subjectivism or bias. Rather it is the removal of prejudice and ill-will, the 'darkness of the mind' by the Spirit in order to see the data for what they are.

But is it not legalistic to look to oneself rather than to Christ for assurance? Is this not reintroducing by the back door a subtle form of salvation by human effort? Does such scrutiny not turn a person back in upon himself in a man-centred way when he should be turned outward to Christ? The charges implicit in these questions would be plausible if what was being suggested was that a person must *place his trust* in his own state of mind or conduct or experience. This *would* be a form of salvation by human works and effort of an obvious kind. But this is not what is being said. There is a world of difference between a person *trusting* in his own state of mind or attainments for salvation and a person *paying attention* to his own states of mind *as evidence that he has been and is converted*.

Each of us has a birthday. A person may for one reason or another, such as old age or forgetfulness, forget what the year of his birth was. In his ignorance he may come to be assured that the year of his birth was, say, 1932 by being shown his birth certificate. But this does not mean that in some strange way his birth certificate becomes a substitute for his birth. His birth at a particular date in the past is fixed. A birth certificate is a generally reliable piece of evidence that his birth was on that particular date. In a similar way a person's conversion is one thing while his *evidence* that he is converted is another. In being converted he trusts Christ for salvation from sin. This is part of what being converted *means*. That person may gain evidence that he is converted, that he is trusting Christ for salvation, from his own experience. But this does not mean that he is trusting himself for salvation. It means that what he finds in himself is important evidence that he is trusting Christ for salvation, as the birth certificate is evidence that a person was born at a particular date in the past.

It is vitally important therefore to distinguish between the reality, faith, and the awareness of the reality, assurance. Faith in Christ alone is the reality. Such faith alone justifies. But the faith that justifies is accompanied by other graces such as repentance. And a person may gain the assurance that he has saving faith from the evidence provided by such other graces. But the presence of this evidence and his use of it does not impair the genuineness nor compromise the simplicity of his faith in Christ.

So faith is reliance upon Christ in order to be saved, not the belief that a person is already saved, and faith is distinct from assurance. But now a further problem arises. If not everyone is saved and the Bible does not contain a list or directory of the names of all those who are saved how can the gospel be offered freely and sincerely? How can it be offered if no one can be told, specifically, 'Christ died for you'?

It has already been seen that if a person could be given this specific information directly, then the nature of saving faith would be drastically altered, even if it did not disappear altogether. This matter may now be left to one side. But how can the gospel be offered freely and sincerely if no one can be told directly that Christ died for him?

When the gospel is proclaimed it is offered *indiscriminately*. It is offered to *anyone* who cares to receive it upon the terms on which it is offered. It is not offered to Mr

Smith or Mrs Robinson because they are Mr Smith or Mrs Robinson, nor to the old or young or rich or poor or black or white because they have these characteristics. It is offered indiscriminately and in this sense universally. Understood in this way the gospel offer is made sincerely. Anyone who comes to Christ will be received. Christ will give rest to any weary one who comes to Him for rest. Furthermore, not only is this indiscriminateness part of the free offer of the gospel, it is a *necessary* part of it. It is necessary that the gospel be proposed for acceptance in general terms in order that salvation may be by faith in Christ. For if it were known that all men without exception were saved, faith in Christ would be unnecessary and the whole nature of a person's acceptance with God and the way in which that acceptance is received would be altered. Or if a list of those for whom salvation was intended had been published in Scripture, then a person would only need to run his eye down the list to check that his name was there to receive assurance, or if it was not there, to become despairing. In neither alternative, neither in that of universalism nor the list, could the biblical way of salvation by faith alone in Christ be preserved and upheld. And so not only is the indiscriminate offer of the gospel possible, given the nature of saving faith and assurance, the indiscriminate offer of the gospel is essential to maintain the character of the gospel.

This is what Calvin meant when he referred to Christ as the 'mirror' of personal election. A person does not gain the knowledge that he is one of the elect through speculating about the names on God's list but through the God-ordained way of salvation by Christ. By the reality of coming to Christ in genuine conversion a person comes to know indirectly that he is one of God's elect, chosen before the foundation of the world.

But does not the call of Christ in the gospel to the needy,

the weary and the heavy laden, mean that certain qual-
ifications are required to come to him? And does this not –
once again – introduce the spectre of salvation by works?
No. Being weary and heavy laden is not a meritorious
work; it is the spiritual condition of the person who has
forsaken the attempt to merit God's favour by his own
deeds. Furthermore, what being weary and heavy laden
means is having the desire to receive Christ as Saviour as
He is set forth in Scripture. It means in effect that those
who have a need for Christ as Saviour – as He is described
in Scripture, and not a Saviour of a mythical kind, a
human invention – are invited to come to Him freely and
without further ado. And what could be freer than that?

MECHANICAL GRACE?

According to Scripture Christian conversion is the work of
God. The strands of the experience of conversion –
conviction of sin, faith in Christ, and true repentance – are
jointly the effect of the work of God the Holy Spirit
working together with the word of God. It is the new life
which He imparts in regeneration which leads to new
beliefs, new desires, and new feelings. The Holy Spirit's
work is not restricted merely to proposing or suggesting
certain matters to the mind, or to prompting a person in a
particular direction, but it extends to the creation of a new
principle or disposition which revives and redirects a
person's deepest characteristics, so that what he once was
indifferent to or despised he now is committed to and
loves. That is why the New Testament with the Old
presents regeneration in radical terms: as a new birth, a
new creation, or a resurrection. It is a change which is the
result of the power of God and which brings life and being
where there was deadness and nothingness and in the
receiving of which the dead soul is passive.

So it is wrong to think of conversion as the decision of a man or as an agreement or contract between a man and God in which grace comes to a man only as the result of his decision to allow it. For one thing such an idea suggests that men before they are converted occupy a position of neutrality or of balance or equilibrium, and that a man by his decision is able to tip the balance one way or the other, to allow grace or to resist it. But any conscious decision, any turning to God, comes about as a result of being turned by God, by being regenerated.

These are theological statements, not descriptions of various accounts of religious experience. This is how conversion is to be accounted for, how it is to be understood, according to Scripture. The conscious experience of one person may be a decision or agreement. It may be that this is how it appears to consciousness: 'I decided for Christ'. Yet to conclude from this that conversion is a decision and nothing more would be to neglect all that Scripture tells us about its source. Experience must be interpreted in the light of Scripture and not *vice versa*.

Regeneration is a giving of life in secret, in the subconscious. And this change in the subconscious, the creation of a 'new man', bears fruit in the conscious life in the creation of new dispositions which lead to new actions. Whereas prior to regeneration there was unbelief, the soul is now disposed to rest on Christ for salvation. Whereas previously there was a contented ignorance, now the soul is disposed to find out all it can from God's revelation about the way of salvation – it is made receptive and teachable. Whereas before there was rebellion, now there is commitment. In this situation what the person is aware of and can only be aware of are the new dispositions. The source of these, the regenerating grace of God the Holy Spirit, remains for ever hidden from consciousness.

[97]

So regeneration, the giving of new life, is an act of God alone which no one can prepare himself to merit or cause to be brought about. But this does not mean that, when a person comes to trust Christ alone for his salvation, it is really God who is believing. Scripture nowhere encourages us to think that God believes for people or repents for them or believes and repents in them. To suppose this would be to verge upon pantheism. It would blur the basic distinction between God and His creatures. When a person believes, the action is *his* action but the ability to believe is a gift from God, one effect of God's regenerating grace.

But does this not represent divine grace as an abstract, almost mechanical force, a force which violates the human personality? There is some misunderstanding in this view, but also something substantive which needs answering. Although so far in the discussion the phrase 'irresistible grace' has not been mentioned the account of conversion that has been given is an account of such grace at work. But what is irresistible grace? The words might suggest a force, like a tidal wave or a battering ram, a force that is so strong that no matter how hard a person tries he cannot overcome it. Or perhaps it suggests a personality so forceful that it always gets its own way. But this is not how irresistible grace is to be thought of. For the irresistibility in question is not necessarily a *felt* irresistibility. It may be. A person may feel God's grace overpowering and subduing him. Perhaps the conversion of Saul of Tarsus is a case of this. But the important point about irresistible grace is not that it is a felt irresistibility, but that it works in the soul to create co-operation and submission where previously there was indifference or rebellion, whether this is created by means of a felt irresistibility or not. The irresistibility in question comes through the creation, the gift of a new heart. The presence of a new heart may manifest itself gently and imperceptibly or through an experience of violent conflict. These psychological differences are important but they do not indicate what irresistible grace means.

Is such irresistible grace impersonal and mechanical? Does it not bypass all our normal decision-making procedures as adult human beings? Are people not being treated by God as things? To these questions there are a number of answers that can be given.

To begin with, such objections do not do justice to the moral depth of conversion. Conversion is a rescue. Just as a would-be rescuer does not wait to consult the unconscious figure floating in the water before rescuing him so God does not consult men about imparting His regenerating, converting grace. And were He to do so, then such is the plight of human beings that no one would listen. Being spiritually dead means being unresponsive to any pleadings or reasonings however powerful or cogent these may be. This rescue takes the form not of a bodily removal from danger but of the imparting of a change in disposition, in belief and intention, at the deepest level of the personality. A desperate situation requires desperate, radical remedies.

It is important not to substitute the biblical models for regeneration and conversion – the model of new birth, of new creation, of resurrection – with other, gentler and less radical models – such as the model of rational discussion, or of partnership. Conversion is not a partnership; it is that which makes partnership possible. It is not a rational discussion with God, 'a little talk with Jesus'; it is that which makes such discussion with God possible.

Furthermore, conversion is the result not of the working of some abstract, impersonal principle, but of *God's* grace. 'Grace' is always God's grace. It is not a purely abstract force but it is God at work, the One who is supremely personal. In the work of regeneration God is bringing to pass what He has designed with supreme love, intelligence and wisdom, and He is doing so in such a way as is best fitted to the personality and situation of the one converted. How God, the eternal Spirit, works upon the spirits of those whom He has created in His own image but who are alienated from Him is a mystery because it is something unparalleled in human experience. But one thing is clear. Such activity is not the cynical manipulation of one individual by another, nor hypnosis, nor, at the other extreme, is it the giving of fatherly advice. It is the restoration of spiritual life – of true human life – the gift of the eternal Spirit.

So divine grace in conversion does not override the human personality or human freedom but rather restores the personality and its freedom (*John 8:36*). As has been emphasised throughout this study it is the purpose of God in conversion to restore men and women to His knowledge and service, to recreate in them the full features of the divine image which was spoilt and lost through sin.

According to Scripture true human freedom is not the freedom to do what one wants to do, unrestrained or unhindered, willy nilly. Such voluntariness is one aspect of freedom but full freedom consists in the knowledge and service of God. No man is free in this sense, however free he may be in other ways, until the Son of God has made him free from the bondage of his own sinful self and personality (*John 8:36*). To bring regenerating and converting grace to someone is to give to him true personal freedom, the freedom of serving God according to His command in a loving and dutiful way.

Part of the mystery of regeneration and conversion – why the human mind cannot fully grasp it – is because while regeneration is the gift of new life, the giving of a 'new man' (*Romans* 7), God so operates in the inner personality that the person in question is not forced against his will nor is his will over-ridden, but he is enabled to consent to and to delight in what previously he had despised and rejected. John Owen says

> There is, therefore, herein an inward almighty *secret act* of the power of the Holy Ghost, producing or effecting in us the will of conversion unto God, so acting our wills as that they also act themselves and that freely. . . The Holy Spirit, who in his power and operation is more intimate, as it were, unto the principles of our souls than they are to themselves, doth, with the preservation and in the liberty of our wills, effectually work our regeneration and conversion unto God.

No one is converted in such a way that he is compelled against his will, but is made willing, and so begins to be a restored person.

The objection that divine grace is mechanical and impersonal surely proceeds from a highly abstract and idealised view of what a human person is. Everyone is continually subject to untold influences of an unconscious and semi-conscious kind, through the matters which are drawn to a person's attention, through human likes and dislikes, the occurrence of apparently chance remarks, and thoughts which arise in the mind seemingly unsought for and unannounced. It is a distorted picture of the human personality to suppose that each person occupies a position of intellectual and moral supremacy over himself, far removed from the effect of such myriad forces. And among such forces are, in God's mercy, His regenerating and converting influences, powerfully but secretly at work in the inner recesses of the personality, yet having an immediate and infallible effect in the thought, belief and conduct of the one who is regenerated.

THE PREACHING OF THE LAW

It has been seen that in the experience of Christian conversion it is usual for saving faith and true repentance to be preceded by a period of the conviction of sin. This is usual, but the Bible does not teach that only those are true conversions which have this preparatory phase of experience. It would be unwise to assume such preparatory work in every instance of true conversion given in the Bible where it is not explicitly mentioned. It is all too easy to fall into ways of thinking which are legalistic in that they look for features of Christian experience that the Bible does not require, and distract from the main thing, namely, coming to Christ in repentance and faith.

Yet there is an appropriateness in the idea of a preparatory work of the conviction of sin because it is only from such an awareness that Christ's office as Saviour from sin is understood and appreciated. It is possible to give the word 'Christ' any meaning and so it is extremely important to gain a proper understanding of who the true Christ is – of His character and work – from Scripture. Is He a political liberator? Is He a divine friend? Is He an inspired teacher? He is, according to Scripture, primarily and pre-eminently the divine Saviour from sin, who denied Himself other tasks (*Luke 12:14*) in order to give Himself unreservedly to this one work. A person will only gain a personal appreciation of this and come to see what Christ has done if he is aware of his need as a sinner in the sight of God. And 'conviction of sin' is a way of expressing this dawning realisation of need before God, the need for forgiveness and righteousness. And so it is difficult to see how someone can come to Christ who has not some inkling of his own need of the Saviour.

A person may not realise at the time that his experience is the experience of the conviction of sin. He may not be familiar with this terminology nor accustomed to the theological and spiritual discrimination that goes with it. And as has been noted he may not in any case be able clearly to distinguish that phase of his experience from other phases which merge with it and overlay it. Nevertheless faith in Christ as Saviour from sin is only made intelligible if it is supposed that the one coming to Christ for salvation has an awareness of his sin. Why else would he trust Christ?

But should there be, corresponding to the experience of the conviction of sin, a distinct 'preaching of the law' in Christian proclamation and witnessing? Should there be in the presentation of the Christian message, and prior to any mention of the office and work of Christ as the only Saviour of sinners, a distinct presentation of the law in all its fulness and spirituality in order to break up the ground – to remove complacency and to show people the holiness of God and of His standards, in order that they might be made aware of how far short they fall of those standards? Should there be a rigid and formal separation of the law and the gospel – the law to convict, the gospel to bring to faith and true repentance?

As a general rule it is wise to be very cautious about such a sharp division between the law and the gospel. To start with, it is hard to see how such a separation would be practicable. But perhaps such hesitations are to be overridden by the clear teaching of Scripture regarding the priority of the preaching of the law over against the preaching of the gospel. For does not Paul clearly say that the law was our school-master to bring us to Christ (*Gal. 3:24*)? Is not Paul here teaching the priority of the law in preaching? This claim is frequently made. But it is hard to see on a correct view of the passage that this is in fact what Paul means.

In this passage in Galatians Paul is arguing *historically*. He is showing that those are the true children of Abraham who are 'of faith' (*v. 7*), who trust God for righteousness. There is, Paul goes on to say, an absolute opposition between such trust and attempts to procure salvation by the works of the law. No one can be justified by the law and all who fail to keep the law fall under its curse. Furthermore, the promise to Abraham that in his seed should all nations be blessed came before the law. Therefore it has priority over the law. The law cannot cancel the promises and therefore those who trust to the law for their salvation are not truly the children of Abraham.

But if the law only brings a curse and if the covenant of Abraham has priority over the law why did the law enter at all? What is its purpose? Paul says it had a temporary, historical purpose. 'It was added because of transgressions, till the seed (Christ) should come to whom the promise was made' (*v. 19*). And in this sense the law was the 'schoolmaster' to the Jewish people, designed to restrain them from sin, to enable them to retain their own national identity as the chosen people of God, and to provide a typical foreshadowing of the Messiah who was to come. The law was the schoolmaster of the Jews in their Mosaic, historical era. But now that Christ has come and the full character of God's grace is revealed in Him the law is no longer necessary. Prior to Christ the Jews 'were in bondage under the elements of the world' (*4:3*), but now that Christ has come, now that God has sent forth His Son and His Spirit (*4:4,6*) the people of God no longer have the character of servants (as they did in the Old Testament) but of sons (*4:7*).

So Paul is discussing the history of God's redeeming purposes, the relationship between the Mosaic economy and the coming of Christ, and not the place of the preaching of the law in the experience of an individual Christian.

Another biblical argument sometimes used is the saying of the risen Christ to Paul on the road to Damascus, 'It is hard for thee to kick against the pricks' (*Acts 9:5*), the assumption being that Christ is here referring to Paul's experience of attempting to subdue the prickings of a conscience awakened by the law. This is a possible interpretation but it is more likely that these words refer to Christ's lordship over Paul.

So it is hard to see how the 'preaching of the law' as a separate phase of preaching can be justified from Scripture in so many words. The conclusion to be drawn is that no rigid rule can be laid down about it. Any faithful preaching of the Christian message will contain elements of both law and gospel. There may be periods in the life of a congregation, or more general situations in the church in which it is necessary that the law be preached fully and unremittingly in order to attempt to convince people that they cannot please God by their own efforts. But in a parallel way there may be periods in which when there is a general feeling of hopelessness and despair the promises and comforts of the gospel should be preached more prominently.

Furthermore, it is a mistake to think that the demands of the law can only be set forth in the preaching of the law as distinct from the gospel. Consider, for example, the character of Christ, His sinlessness. This will form a part of any proper preaching of the gospel: Christ is the spotless lamb, the immaculate Saviour who knew no sin. His sinlessness can hardly be set forth without making clear the character of sin and of the law. Or consider the nature of Christ's atonement. It is a satisfaction of divine justice through which sinners are forgiven. Again, it is hard to see how the true nature of the atonement can be made clear without making clear at the same time the character of the need – guilt, the need for forgiveness and reconciliation – that the atonement is designed to meet. Or finally, consider the sanctifying work of the Holy Spirit, His work in renewing the character of men and women in the image of God. It is hard to see how the precise character of this work of the Holy Spirit can be set forth without mentioning the nature of true holiness in God and man and thus setting out the nature of the divine law as giving the pattern of acceptable living before God.

And so at each point law and gospel are intertwined, since the nature of the gospel can only be understood together with an understanding of the divine law. The gospel is shot through with law, not in the sense that the gospel is a new law, but in the sense that the categories of law – transgression, guilt, pollution – are needed to make clear the precise character of the work the Saviour came to perform.

SUMMARY

Christian conversion, properly understood, is not legalistic. It does not lay down conditions for salvation. Rather the faith by which a person trusts Christ is brought about in a certain kind of situation with certain accompaniments. In order to avoid misunderstanding it is preferable to think of *strands* in conversion rather than *stages* through which any converted person must pass. Further, there is no incompatibility between the understanding of conversion, particularly the distinction between faith and assurance, and the free offer of the gospel. The effectual call of God in conversion is not a mechanical effect of an impersonal principle but the renewing of people by the personal agency of God. Finally, though the preaching of the law should be given prominence along with the preaching of the gospel, for the gospel cannot be understood without the presupposition of the divine law, nevertheless it would be wrong to think that 'the law' must be preached in a way which is separate and distinct from the preaching of the gospel.

5: *Some Consequences*

The great change that must happen to all who are to become Christians has certain essential strands – the conviction of sin, faith in Christ, and a turning from sin to God in repentance. In the previous chapter an attempt was made to meet certain objections before glancing at some wider consequences of the change. How does a proper understanding of conversion provide, in turn, an understanding of the connection between Christ's work *for* men (appropriated by faith alone for their justification) and His work *in* men (their sanctification)? And what does a proper understanding of conversion teach about the character of Christian piety and spirituality?

JUSTIFICATION AND SANCTIFICATION

Scripture teaches that a person's justification before God is by faith alone. It is as he trusts Christ the redeemer that the believer receives pardon (*1 John 1:9*), reconciliation, (*2 Cor. 5:18–20*), and peace with God (*Rom. 5:1*). Faith relies upon another, Jesus Christ. Although Christ procured atonement for the church almost two thousand years ago, and so then procured their justification by His death (*1 Cor. 1:23*) and especially by His resurrection (*Rom. 4:24,25*), yet this objective atonement is not personally and individually applied and enjoyed until a person reaches out in God-given faith to Christ. So while Christ objectively procured justification for His people many years ago no one can know who exactly He died for except by discovering who believes.

Justification is by faith alone but this faith is not to be thought of as a work of the believer, his own achievement, something of which he may be proud. It is this fact, the *aloneness* of saving faith, which makes as clear as it is possible to make it that salvation is God's gift to sinners. Salvation – the forgiveness of sins and the imputing of Christ's righteousness to the ungodly – is wholly God's work, received by the God-given hand of faith.

The proclaiming of justification by faith alone, although it has been central both to the distinctive emphasis of the Protestant Reformation and more importantly to a proper understanding of the biblical gospel, has sometimes been the source of some misunderstanding and difficulty. Does not telling men and women that they are justified by faith alone encourage ungodly living? If all that is required for a person's salvation was accomplished by Christ two thousand years ago what need is there for an upright life? Is it not perfectly consistent for someone who rests on Christ by faith to fold his hands, or to do as he pleases, without regard to any moral standards? If he is justified by faith may not the believer live as he likes since nothing that he now does can add to what Christ has done (since Christ has done everything necessary) and since nothing that he now does can detract from what Christ has done (since Christ has done everything necessary)?

The Roman Catholic Church was not slow to make precisely this criticism of the Reformers' understanding of justification, and to charge the Reformation teaching on justification by faith alone with encouraging *antinomianism*, or as it might be expressed today, permissiveness. And from the opposite, radical wing of Christianity the conclusion that justified sinners are 'free from the law', and so free to please themselves, has often been welcomed and emphasised as a precious aspect of Christian liberty.

What is to be said to these charges? If justification (the removal of guilt, the imputation of righteousness) and sanctification (the renewal of people in the image of God) are separated, can they ever be put back together again?

It is precisely this problem of antinomianism which Paul faced in Romans. (And, incidentally, the fact that the problem arose as an objection to his preaching of the gospel is one powerful piece of evidence that he taught justification by faith alone as the Reformation came later to understand it.) Paul answered the objection by stressing the believer's *personal union* with Christ in His death and resurrection (*Rom. 6:3–5*). It is because of this union that the believer is to reckon himself 'dead indeed unto sin, but alive unto God' (*Rom. 6:11*), not to let sin reign in his body to fulfil it in lust, but to yield (that is, to consecrate) himself to God as one who is alive from the dead with Christ.

This is one way in which Scripture answers the charge of antinomianism. But there is another way which our study of conversion should make clear and which can now be drawn out explicitly. Faith is one element, the central element in the moral and spiritual change of conversion. Faith is not an off-the-cuff decision nor is it a leap in the dark but it is part of a deep change. And although faith alone saves, faith is never in fact separable from the other elements of conversion, conviction of sin and repentance.

So terms like 'faith', 'repentance' and 'conviction of sin' are not simply words. There is a world of difference between talking about love and loving, or talking about cancer and having cancer, and there is a world of difference between talking about faith and believing. It is important that people do talk about love, and about cancer and saving faith. It is important that people think as clearly and steadily about saving faith as it is possible to do, and to do this it is necessary to consider the idea of saving faith abstractly. But a proper concern to think clearly should not encourage the thought that these ideas are merely tokens, pieces to be moved about on a theological chessboard. They express lived realities for countless thousands of people.

While faith, repentance and conviction of sin are each separable in thought and in discussion, having different meanings and different theological values (while faith saves, conviction of sin does not, for example), nevertheless they are inseparable in true Christian experience. Truly to experience repentance before God involves truly experiencing and possessing faith in Christ. Though every coin must have two sides, it is possible to distinguish between the 'heads' side of it and the 'tails' side and to discuss the distinctive shape of each without in any way involving the other. Similarly, it is possible to discuss repentance apart from faith even though true repentance can never exist apart from faith. Every believer is a penitent believer and every true penitent is a believing penitent.

It is important to think this through as it affects Christian conversion. Faith and repentance are inseparable in true Christian experience. In the Christian, conviction of sin has led to a deep-seated judgment about the moral character of his life, to repentance, a change of mind. As long as faith endures such a verdict of the believer on himself will endure. If he were to cease to be penitent he would cease to be a believer. It therefore follows that it is impossible to be a true believer and to be indifferent to the moral character of one's desires, intentions and public behaviour. To suppose otherwise, to suppose that a believer could be morally careless and carefree, is to suppose that faith could become morally indifferent or morally neutral, and this is to suppose that it could be disconnected from repentance. This is impossible. Faith without works is 'dead, being alone' (*Jas. 2:17*). Or, in other words, faith without works is not true faith.

And so the saving faith of a Christian possesses a definite and inseparable moral character. The believer cannot consistently repudiate his old life and turn to God, which is what repentance is, while at the same time still clinging to his old life. But may not a believer be inconsistent? May he not fall, and fail? He may and will, because his renewed moral and spiritual abilities are not completely healed. (This is one of the lessons of Romans 7.) But at the deepest level his resolve to live to please God remains undiminished even though through weakness he fails. (This is another lesson of Romans 7.)

Furthermore, not only does a proper understanding of Christian conversion reinforce the inseparability of justification and sanctification in experience, it also underlines what the standard of true sanctification is. As conviction of sin is brought about by the law of God placed against the individual's life, and saving faith is faith in Christ as the divine guilt-bearer and bringer of righteousness, and repentance is turning from sin to God, so the standard of sanctification is that same law of God. The degree of sanctification is not to be gauged by a person's own aspirations, or by the conduct and standards of the surrounding society, but by the law of God revealed in its true fulness by Christ (*Matt. 5–7*) and by His apostles (e.g. *Rom. 13:8–10, Gal. 5:13,14*).

The linkage in experience between faith, conviction of sin and repentance also affords a proper understanding of the idea that once a person is a believer he will never cease to be one, a fact sometimes expressed in the slogan 'Once saved, always saved'. Is this slogan true? The New Testament is emphatic that it is (*John 10:27–9, Phil. 1:6*). But this endorsement must be properly understood. The New Testament does not teach that all who think they are saved are saved (*Matt. 7:21, 22*), nor does it teach that all who make a profession of faith are always saved (*John. 2:19*), but what it does teach is that all who are once truly saved are saved for all time. And the idea of perseverance in the faith embodied in the slogan ought not to be considered apart from the dynamics of the Christian faith. A person is saved, and continues to be saved, so long as he actually perseveres with a true faith. Someone with a true faith will desire to continue, and will continue, not because of human determination or grittiness but because of what faith is. The warnings and encouraging promises of the New Testament (for example, in the letter to the Hebrews (*Heb. 4*)) are not to be thought of as conveying the possibility that someone with true faith might actually fall away, fail to persevere, but rather as conveying the thought that a true believer will conscientiously pay attention to such warnings and encouragements, allow himself to be 'steered' by them, and so persevere. From God's own perspective the believer is enabled to persevere by being granted renewed faith, according to promise, apart from which he would depart from God. This is not because 'faith' is a mystical or magical ingredient but because loss of faith *is* departure from God.

The slogan 'Once saved, always saved' is being misused when someone infers from it that 'Since a person is saved he can do what he likes because God will keep him and save him at the last', just as it is being misused when someone argues, 'Since I once made a profession of faith, I am a believer now'.

But if, in order to persevere in the faith, a person has to

be continuing actively in the faith, in sanctification, what is the point of Scripture insisting upon perseverance? What value does it have? The answer is that the promise of perseverance is a comfort to the *weak* believer, someone who is faithful but who is plagued by doubts and whose own weakness is apparent to himself. Such a person may ask, 'Will I hold out to the end? Will God keep me?' And to these questions the answer is 'Yes', for that is what the divinely revealed promise of perseverance states. He who begins a 'good work' in His people will continue it 'until the day of Jesus Christ' (*Phil. 1:6*). As with all doctrines it is possible to abuse the teaching on perseverance. But the remedy for such abuse is not to abandon the doctrine or water it down but to pay attention to its proper uses.

THE IMPORTANCE OF CHRISTIAN EXPERIENCE

One theme of the earlier chapters was the importance for the Christian of ensuring that his experience of God is properly interpreted, understood and evaluated in the light of Scripture. Scripture must control experience and not *vice versa*. Because of the primacy of Scripture in interpreting and evaluating Christian experience it ought not to be regarded merely as 'religious experience', something vague, but as 'Christian experience', something having a distinctive form and character shaped by God's revelation. It is the product of God's grace, with Christ as its focus and object. It is now possible to see the importance of Christian experience more clearly.

In the first place the truth of God embodied and expressed in the gospel must be *experienced*. The truth of God is objective truth and like all objective truth it stands whatever our own attitude towards it may be. The truths of divine revelation do not depend for their truth upon our upbringing, our culture or our vote. They are not culturally conditioned in such a way as to be only relatively true, true in one set of circumstances and false in another set.

Yet in order that an individual may personally benefit from God's truth, that truth must be personally appropriated. God's goodness must be *tasted* (*Ps. 34:8*). As it is impossible for you to give me the taste of a pineapple if you alone eat it – I must eat the pineapple myself in order to get the taste – so a person does not benefit personally from God's truth unless he recognises it, unless he gives it its full weight and responds appropriately to it in thorough conviction of sin, repentance and faith with all the emotional and ethical upheaval this may bring. A person who feels deeply his plight before God and who delights in God's gracious deliverance through Christ cannot be accused of enthusiasm or emotionalism. For he is moved by the truth, truth about God and about himself.

It is in this sense that biblical Christianity has an intensely personal centre – a man's relationship to his Maker and Judge through Christ. Even though his Christian faith should and does show itself in theological reflection and research, and in social relationships, in the family, at work, and in leisure and other cultural pursuits in society, these cannot replace an individual's relationship with God, his personal appropriation of and experience of God's grace through Christ. These other activities derive their point, their strength and their distinctive character from this personal walk with God.

In the second place the fact of such personal Christian experience is an important strand of evidence for the truth of the Christian faith. The question of how people are to be convinced of the truth of the Christian revelation, particularly if they come from a non-Christian background, has concerned theologians ever since the death of the apostles, and numerous proposals have been made. Some have said that the truth of the Christian revelation is established by human reason, while others have appealed to the historical credibility and trustworthiness of the revelation. Some have appealed to the authority of the church while still others have insisted that faith authenticates itself.

It would be rash to dismiss any of these lines of argument out of hand. A revelation that was manifestly logically incoherent could hardly be from the God of truth, nor could a revelation that claimed to reveal what has taken place in history retain credibility if it could be shown to be historically baseless. It could hardly be the case that Jesus Christ was crucified under Pontius Pilate if there never was such a man or if he had lived a hundred years earlier or later.

Among these various lines of evidence individual Christian experience has an important and an often underestimated place. It goes without saying that the experience of one person or of countless people cannot alter the truth. If Jesus Christ was not crucified then the existence of a million people who are convinced that He was crucified will not change history. Christianity is not true or even credible simply because countless people have believed that it is credible.

So personal experience cannot change history or objective truth of any kind. Yet one important feature of the Christian gospel is that it is not an abstract or theoretical set of doctrines or historical facts, but that it makes claims which hold good when put to the test in the everyday lives of people, of anyone. The diagnosis of human need in Scripture, the warnings about human plight before God, and the invitations to people to find forgiveness and new life in Christ, are found to hold true for all those who take these words seriously and who respond to them appropriately. Just as one way in which a doctor establishes his skill is in the making of accurate diagnoses, diagnoses which are found to hold good in fact, so the credibility of the gospel is to be established not only by rational argument or historical investigation, important as these are, but by the personal experience of its converting and liberating effects. For if the Christian gospel is true these effects will be found in human lives into which the gospel comes. And the fact that they are found to occur gives general credibility to the claims of the gospel. The fact that not every one finds the good news acceptable has an explanation (e.g. *John 5:44*), but whoever comes to Jesus will under no circumstances be turned away (*John 6:35, 37*).

In the third place Christian experience of God's grace is important as an evidence to others of the credibility and reality of what Christians profess to believe. This is a repeated theme of the New Testament. The reality of the truth is seen in changed lives. And the New Testament writers repeatedly draw attention to the inconsistency and hollowness of professing one thing and doing another (e.g. *Matt. 23:13–28*).

CHRISTIAN PIETY

So Christian conversion is not only the formal adoption of a creed, of a framework of belief, important as such creeds and frameworks are. It implies a deep change in the moral and spiritual direction of the person converted. This is the initial, decisive change in that person's becoming a member of God's new humanity under Christ.

The piety of a converted person is *God-centred*. The converted person depends upon the word of God, God's revelation. The importance of this was shown earlier – the word of God in convincing a person of his sin by showing him God's standards from which he has fallen, and that same word of God bringing the message of deliverance through Christ. Although someone may have through his conscience a vague inkling of his responsibility before God, yet it is only through divine revelation that he can come to understand this responsibility clearly. Such revelation is God's objective disclosure – through prophets, evangelists and apostles, and supremely in His Son – of matters which would otherwise be hidden and unknown to anyone. It is truth disclosed by God's gracious decision, truth about God's own redemptive action in Jesus Christ. The converted person comes to know God through this revelation and he depends upon it as God's permanent 'message' to him throughout the rest of his life.

Revelation in this sense is clearly the complete opposite of human discovery and speculation. It is truth that is not uncovered or stumbled upon by men but intentionally disclosed by God. A person whose faith is centred in the word of God, who depends upon it for the knowledge of God and of himself is, if he is consistent, invariably going to be God-centred in his thought. He is aware that he depends upon God and on what God has willed to disclose and to do.

His piety is God-centred in another way in that he sees his life as a *response to God*. It is certainly not the case that the converted person regards himself as emancipated from God, as a secular man 'come of age' (whatever this may mean). He knows himself to be bound to God, depending upon Him for His mercy and grace in daily forgiveness and in the struggle against remaining sin.

Such a God-centred piety is to be contrasted with religion which consists very largely in morality and social action. In such a religious outlook devotion to God becomes obscured or forgotten, or reinterpreted as devotion to men and to various causes. The converted person certainly ought not to be oblivious to the needs of his fellow-men or to neglect opportunities for social and political action any more than he ought to turn his back on all scientific research or technological change. But such concerns are to be expressed as part of his devotion to God and not as a substitute for it. It is in this way that the converted person is to be a biblical humanist. The converted person's attitude to such activities is guided by the basic principles of the word of God about human sinfulness, the frailty of human institutions, the human tendency to exaggerate and polarise and to swing between extremes, as well as by the specific directives of Scripture about family life and human culture.

Such piety is *moral*. Conversion is the decisive step in the experience of an individual in the restoration of his true humanity, humanity which is to be understood in terms of the knowledge and service of God. This service is grateful obedience to the law of God, not obedience in order to merit or gain the favour of God, but obedience because Christ has obtained God's favour for the sinner, and the sinner is grateful. How is this obedience to be understood? In terms of the service of God and man, not as two conflicting or potentially conflicting aims or objectives but as brought into harmony in God's law. It is not the service of God at the expense of the service of man, or *vice versa*. It is the service of men because it is part of God's will that this be so.

So the converted person does not withdraw from society. His piety is not individualistic to the point where no-one else matters. For other people – his family, his neighbours, his fellow-countrymen – are like himself made in the image of God and he is commanded by God to love his neighbour as himself. The restoration of God's image in man is expressed in such love. It is not that the restoration of God's image in man *consists in* love to the neighbour, but it is shown by love to the neighbour for Christ's sake. And so the Christian will try to promote love and justice within society, among his family, and his friends, and within the wider circle of his acquaintances, and even extending to those whom he has never seen.

Furthermore, such piety is *culturally aware*. Part of what it meant, originally, to be made in the image of God, is seen in what has been called the 'cultural mandate' from God, a command to cultivate and subdue the earth for God's glory (*Gen. 1:28*). In being converted to God and having God's image restored in him by God's word and Spirit, the converted man will wish to take up in a proper fashion that cultural calling which has become perverted through human sin. This calling is expressed in philosophy, science, politics, the arts and literature, in daily work and leisure. To the extent that participation in these activities is not unlawful the converted person is to foster them. He has been given no detailed blueprint for success, and often in cultural as in moral matters he has to struggle with his own perverse and ignorant nature and an inherited culture which is twisted by human sin.

Finally, Christian piety is *directed to the end-time*, the consummation of all things, when God's kingdom will finally be revealed publicly in its full splendour and glory. And so the converted person does not look for his final satisfaction and fulfilment in this life but in the life beyond the grave, life in the full presence of God, a life which, because it is shrouded in mystery, can only at present be dimly discerned.

WORD AND SPIRIT ONCE AGAIN

The word of God and the Spirit of God combine together in conversion. Conversion is not due to 'spirit' alone, an emotional enthusiasm in which a person 'blows his mind'. Rather conversion is rooted in an awareness of the truth. But it is not, in turn, a mere intellectualism, a case of being fascinated by certain ideas. It is the word of God to a man's mind and heart brought home by the power of the Holy Spirit. So strong is this connection between word and spirit that a converted person's understanding of himself is bound up with certain thought-forms. The various strands or elements of conversion discussed earlier are not simply a way of describing experience based upon personal preference or historical tradition. To suppose that a person may simply choose to regard a certain change in his life as a 'conversion' suggests that someone else might legitimately describe the same experience in other ways. Rather, a person's understanding of himself and his integrity as a converted person are bound up with this particular understanding of the change which has come upon him at conversion. If he could be persuaded by the evidence that when he was 'converted' he had not really trusted Christ for salvation and repented before God, then the whole character of his experience and of how he understands himself would be changed.

Suppose, for example, that a converted person could be persuaded that there was no such thing as sin against God and that to talk of 'sin' in this way is a figment of a diseased religious imagination. If there is no sin, then the converted person could no longer regard himself as being under conviction of sin and another explanation of his beliefs and feelings would have to be sought. If there is no sin, then there is no need for a divine Saviour to procure atonement for sin by His death. If the converted person came to regard what he had previously thought of as conviction of sin as merely personal inadequacy of some kind, which could be overcome by one of various means – by therapy, or education, by being given a greater degree of responsibility at work, or whatever – then it would follow that he had come to understand himself in a fundamentally different way from the way in which he understood himself before.

For illustration, suppose someone comes to regard marriage not as the joining of man and wife in lifelong union in the sight of God but as a civil contract to be entered into freely and renounced when one or other finds, or both of them find it desirable or convenient to do so. It is perhaps tempting to suppose that here are two different ways of understanding the same thing – marriage. But this would be mistaken. Rather, here are *two different concepts of marriage*. It is not that there is some one thing – marriage – which it is possible to understand in two or more different ways, but there are two (or more) different concepts of marriage, no doubt with certain similarities or common features. So that someone who believed himself to be getting married in the first sense would have a markedly different understanding from someone who regarded himself as getting married in the second sense. He would see himself and his partner and the nature of their life together in quite different terms from the other. (Think how commercialism in sport has changed it from recreation into big business.)

So it is with Christian conversion. To be converted to Christ is not to have some vague or general experience which one chooses to interpret as a conversion and which someone else may choose to interpret differently. The language in which the experience of conversion is thought about and understood, the language of divine revelation, is *part of* that experience. Coming to believe that one is converted is coming to accept a whole web or network of beliefs about oneself in relation to God, beliefs about the nature of God, about one's past, about one's future, and much more. And so it is impossible to draw a sharp line of demarcation between Christian doctrine and experience. It is not, as it has become almost a commonplace of modern theology to think, that Christian doctrine is constructed out of 'religious experience'. It is rather that

Christian doctrine, in order to be acceptable and accepted, must interpret experience and bear the weight of that experience, and the experience of God's grace is unintelligible apart from that grace.

From this it is possible to see what happens at times of religious declension and of religious revival. One of the things that may happen is that individuals or a whole community no longer think of themselves as responsible to God and as being sinners in need of a Saviour. There may be various reasons for this, but the upshot of such an attitude is that the whole idea of Christ, the eternal Son of God, being a divine Saviour from sin is put to one side. Either belief in Christ is abandoned altogether, or it is continued in purely notional terms, or the person and work of Christ is reinterpreted in a way that is compatible with a person's new beliefs about himself. (The decay of evangelicalism in many families throughout the second half of the nineteenth century may be understood in these terms.) In the case of revival, a previously careless person may come to regard himself as morally responsible to God not only for his actions but for his thoughts and desires and his general moral disposition. And as a result of this he may come to believe that the Christ whom previously he had scorned or ignored or taken for granted, or about whom he had entertained all sorts of misconceptions, is the only person who can mediate between himself and the God whom he has offended. Such a change in outlook may happen to an entire community.

OUR LANGUAGE

The strong connection between Christian doctrine and the character of Christian experience is one reason why it is not a light thing to propose changes in Christian doctrine or even in its customary forms of expression. For

Christian doctrine forms a conceptual scheme, a web of understanding of the whole of life in which each aspect is interrelated with all others. To propose changes can easily result in distortion. But more than this, Christian doctrine gives Christian experience its true character. So while Christian conversion and the Christian life as a whole admit of a wide variety of individual experiences, they are composed of certain fixed elements or strands and to propose alterations in these strands is to tamper with the whole nature of Christian piety.

For example, suppose it is said that there is no distinction between saving faith and assurance, and consequently that anyone who thinks that he believes in fact does so. Such a person is taught to think that all doubts and strains in his faith in Christ must at once be dismissed as due to a misunderstanding of what faith is. He thinks that there is no possibility of self-deception. If this person lives out these convictions consistently he will have an entirely different view of what faith is, and a characteristically different piety, from a person for whom the possibilities of self-deception, doubt and spiritual darkness are realities. For this person faith is faith that Christ has saved me. For him any doubts on the matter are unbelief, they could never provide proper grounds for caution or occasions for self-examination before God. Such doubts are never legitimate but are always improper.

What about the recognition of guilt before God? Ought a person to believe that he is guilty because he has broken the law of God, and to experience penitence and contrition as a consequence? Are these legitimate expressions of Christian piety? Or ought he to banish such thoughts with the counter-thought that God loves him because God loves everyone, and that faith is the acceptance of this love? Someone who thinks that a feeling of deep penitence is no part of proper Christian experience has a very different concept of what a Christian is from someone else who regards it as inseparable from being a Christian. And likewise those who, paying attention to the New Testament warnings to watch (*Col. 4:2, I Thess. 5:6*) and to fear (*Phil. 2:12*), and about the nature and possibility of self-deception (*I Cor. 6:9, Jas. 1:26*), wonder whether their conviction of sin is genuine or not, will have a different conception of what it means to be a Christian from someone who thinks that conviction of sin ought to play little or no part in the life of a Christian.

For those whose Christian experience is formed through (among other things) a belief in God's discriminating love, together with the possibility of being deceived about one's own relationship or standing before God, and the need for a 'law-work', concepts such as self-deception, conviction of sin, and penitence before God are not detachable from what it means to be a Christian. They are part of what being a Christian *is*.

This concern for appropriate language ought also to be reflected in the manner of Christian worship. Christian worship is a distinctive activity and not a mere social occasion or an opportunity for self-indulgent expression. Even allowing for the cultural differences of different communities, worship involves a common recognition by worshippers that they are in the presence of God, the God who has revealed Himself to sinners and who has provided unmerited salvation and grace for those who deserve wrath. Christian worship is for sinners, and it is as sinners that Christians worship. The characteristic expressions of worship are the characteristic expressions of Christian experience – conviction of sin, penitence before God, faith in His mercy, the struggle against unbelief and weakness, joy and peace in believing and renewed resolve to serve God in glad obedience. The chief mark of such worship is not friendliness, nor 'bright singing', nor theatrical display but serious reflection upon the word of God and the expression in measured terms of the deepest responses of the soul to God in prayer and praise. This is the common liturgy of the Christian church.

There is at present an increasing emphasis in evangelical churches on informality in worship both in its manner and its language and on the frank sharing of personal feelings in public. Someone who thinks that each of us has an accurate knowledge of himself and that we should always say frankly what we feel will see nothing but gain in such a development. But someone who is impressed by what Scripture says about the difficulty of knowing one's own inner motives and desires and who has been made aware of this in his own experience will be much more cautious. Talkativeness is not necessarily a sign of great knowledge or wisdom and the very willingness to talk in public about deeply personal matters can itself introduce distortion and a further layer of self-deceit. To a person who is aware of his own capacity for self-deception the emphasis on 'frankness' will appear to have more in common with the modern fondness for explicitness and the modern quest for 'authenticity' than with Christian principle.

Because of the strong connection between the word of God and the Spirit of God and the vital place that human understanding plays in coming to Christ, a distorted presentation of the gospel will in all likelihood produce distorted Christian experience. And so teaching in which no distinction is made between saving faith and the assurance of faith will produce professing Christians who cannot register this distinction in their own experience because they are not aware of it. If no one knows what measles is then no one will be diagnosed as having measles. An evangelistic proclamation of the faith which dispenses with the elements of conviction of sin and penitence, whose essential message is 'Jesus loves us – Come to Jesus' will produce converts whose experiences of conviction of sin and of penitence are either smothered or explained away.

A frequent theme of modern theology has been that the Christian faith must be de-mythologised in order to be made relevant and acceptable to modern people. Such a call is radically misconceived. What is needed is not for the Christian faith to be de-mythologised but for people to think their way back into the basic biblical categories. To say this is not to be obscurantist or to want to run away from the twentieth century. It is to reaffirm that it is only in terms of the biblical categories of law and sin, of grace and forgiveness, and of penitence and saving faith, that people can properly understand themselves and the God-given remedy for their plight, and begin to function again as people made in God's image.

There comes a point when a 'modern man' must be prepared to think himself back into the biblical account of things, when, having removed all archaic expressions in that account, he must face up to the distinctively biblical portrayal of himself. To use such concepts as 'conviction of sin', 'repentance', 'faith' and 'assurance' is not to use a merely traditional or out-dated way of describing something which could be understood in other, more modern, and equally valid ways. These concepts are an integral part of the Christian message and of the Christian way of life, of its challenge and its vision.

Epilogue

One of the most pressing needs at present is for the Christian's ideas about conversion and about the whole course of Christian experience to be gained from and controlled by Scripture. It is a sad fact that even those who acknowledge the authority of Scripture and who willingly depend upon Scripture for its teaching upon, for instance, the Person of Christ, or the atonement, are reluctant to allow to Scripture the same authority regarding Christian experience. Sometimes one dominant person's experience is allowed to dictate what the experience of others shall be. Sometimes thinking about such matters is governed by what is in vogue in the general culture. And sometimes a person will allow his own understanding of himself to act as a sieve to emphasise certain features of Scripture and to play down others.

There is a strong appeal in this. Who can deny the reality of what he has experienced for himself? If coming to Jesus has made a person happy, what is easier than to conclude that Jesus came to make people happier? If becoming a Christian has been followed by a successful business career, who dare deny that Jesus came in order to give us success in life? If a person is full of joy so long as he pays no attention to the exact nature of his feelings, who dare say that he ought to pay attention to them?

The appeal to 'experience' is invariably to what is *consciously* experienced, what a person is aware of. But what each of us is aware of about himself is only part of the story. A person may come suddenly to be aware of his need, and come at once to Christ. But it would be wrong to think that everything about conversion is sudden. What about those whose experience is less sudden? What about the influences which led in this case to the sudden change? Could it not be that this person's mind was being imperceptibly prepared over a considerable period of time? Someone else may be aware of the occasion when he first consciously exercised faith in Christ. Perhaps he can vividly recollect the time and the place. But it would be mistaken to infer from this that conversion is essentially a conscious choice and that nothing else counts as conversion. For a person's *conscious* choice may not be his *first* choice. May it not be that his mind was being affected by the gospel long before he recognised the fact?

But while being thoughtful and reflective in this way will help to correct hasty first impressions it will not by itself go very far. As has repeatedly been shown, Scripture is needed to interpret experience. Suppose I see a narrow oblong booklet consisting of pink lined pages all of which seem to be more or less the same. What is it? What is it for? What can I do with it? I cannot answer these questions simply by examining the booklet more thoroughly. If I am to understand that the booklet is a cheque-book then I need to know not only about the booklet itself but also about banking – about bank balances, credit, the honouring of cheques and so forth. What makes the booklet a cheque-book is not only its distinctive shape and printing but also its place in the banking system.

Similarly with Christian experience. What makes a person's trust a case of trusting in Christ, his fear a fear of God, his bad conscience the conviction of sin, his feeling of sorrow true repentance? Feelings and beliefs themselves will not indicate this any more than the pink booklet by itself indicates that it is a cheque-book. They need interpreting in the light of the discriminations made in Scripture and they need to be appropriate responses to one aspect or another of biblical truth. The need for a framework of understanding shows us why it is impossible to do what much modern theology has attempted to do time and time again, to construct a Christian theology using only the materials of human experience. For there is no such thing as raw human experience.

It is because of the close way in which experience and Scripture are and ought to be intertwined that the language that is used in worship, in preaching and in all other forms of Christian communication, ought to be chosen with great care, not only for its beauty and economy (certainly not for its entertainment value), but for its faithfulness to Scripture. Writing about politics and language George Orwell said

> A man may take to drink because he feels himself to be a failure, and then fail all the more completely because he drinks. It is rather the same thing that is happening to the English language. It becomes ugly and inaccurate because our thoughts are foolish, but the slovenliness of our language makes it easier for us to have foolish thoughts.

What Orwell detects about language in general can easily happen in the language of Christians. It may seem to be easier, slicker and less cumbersome to talk of 'Jesus' than of 'the Lord Jesus Christ', of 'coming to Jesus' rather than of 'being called by grace', but such seemingly small and hardly noticed changes can be very significant. They can reveal in the speaker a weak and imprecise grasp of biblical truth. 'The Lord Jesus Christ', the eternal Son of God made flesh, can easily become 'Jesus', a friend. Jesus is a friend, as the Bible teaches. But He is not only a friend, and He is a friend of a rather special kind because

[129]

He is a rather special person. 'Being called by grace' can easily and imperceptibly become 'coming to Jesus', and this can become 'giving my heart to Jesus'. Of course when a person is called by grace he comes to Jesus, and when a person comes to Jesus he gives his heart to Jesus. But there is a loss of definiteness, of biblical fulness and precision in the slide from one expression to another. The language of Christian communication degenerates, though the loss may only fully be felt by sons and daughters.

This degeneration may be for a variety of reasons. It may show imperfect understanding of truth. It may arise from a desire to present the gospel in an appealing and relevant way. But, whatever the reasons for it, the effects of such a decline are disastrous because of the connection between the meaning of what is uttered and the character of the experience of those who respond to the utterance. If the Saviour is presented as 'my friend Jesus', then unless this is corrected those who respond will not be abased at the feet of the divine Saviour from sin, they will make friends with Jesus. And this will condition and impoverish the whole of their experience and self-understanding as Christians. No doubt it is possible to be maddeningly pedantic and archaic in the presentation of the gospel, and this is indefensible. No effort must be spared to engage the minds and hearts of those who are unbelieving, but it must be the gospel in all its fulness that is used to engage them.

Ours is a pluralist society, one which officially favours or at least tolerates a great number of different views of the world, lifestyles and personal ideals. Provided that people observe certain social standards they are permitted by the law to flourish and even in some instances are actively encouraged to 'do their own thing'. Marxists live alongside humanists, conservatives alongside radicals,

Jehovah's Witnesses alongside Roman Catholics, and so on.

For such tolerance the Christian ought to be deeply thankful to God. Freedom of worship is a great blessing. But it is easy to slip into thinking that because a multitude of different views is officially allowed it does not matter which view one takes. Even worse than this is to suppose that such toleration implies that there is no such thing as truth. Religion becomes a matter of individual preference, like choosing ties. Or truth is what you and your group *decide* is true. There is Marxist truth and humanist truth and Hindu truth and Christian truth. Pluralism leads easily to relativism. You can believe what you like and so it does not matter what you believe. If it suits you, if it turns you on, it is true. The toleration of many views may lead people to think that no view can be true or (what comes to very much the same thing) that one view is as true as another.

But what happens when persons are converted? What is beginning? It is not simply that they become happy or powerful or fulfilled. In fact they may become none of these things at conversion. Nor is it that they have simply developed a taste for the Christian religion. They have come to recognise *the truth* about themselves in relation to the eternal God. This truth about their relation to God existed long before they recognised it, in just the same way that the furniture in the room exists before the light is switched on to reveal it. Turning on the light does not create the furniture, it shows it up. In the same way conversion involves a *recognition* of the truth about ourselves, truth which would remain true even if it were not recognised by us. This is why being unconverted is often expressed in Scripture as being in the dark, and the call of God in conversion as the giving of light. Men may not recognise it, but they are estranged from God and

God's eternal Son is the only deliverer from this predicament. Being converted involves recognising this.

Certain things are a matter of taste. You may like coffee and I may like tea. Which preference is correct? There's no way of answering that question. Nothing would settle the difference between us. There is no point in searching for further facts, thinking up experiments, or having an argument. But Christian conversion is not like this. It is being brought by God to recognise the truth about oneself.

Because many are inclined to explain away Christian conversion merely as a matter of personal lifestyle – being religious – it is an important part of the Christian testimony at present to maintain the precise opposite. Christian conversion means being apprehended by God who is the truth and who knows men far better than they know themselves. But there is no prospect of proving to others that this is so. Rather, the biblical way of 'practising the truth' is to maintain a consistent and coherent life which reveals the effect of God's truth in the life. The furniture in the room is revealed by where I sit and where I stand and where I eat. This shows that my talk of the furniture is not a figment of my imagination. The reality of God's truth about me and about the way of my deliverance through Christ is shown in a parallel way.

Conversion is not an irrational emotional reaction, a mindless leap of faith, but it is based upon the truth, God's revealed truth. But someone who is converted does not have a new secret or mystical revelation from God. The objective truth which the Holy Spirit uses in conversion is the truth which is publicly available for any to read and understand. As B. B. Warfield put it:

The Holy Spirit does not work a blind, an ungrounded faith in the heart. What is supplied by his creative energy in working faith is not a ready-made faith, rooted in nothing and clinging without reason to its object; nor yet new grounds of belief in the object presented; but just a new ability of the heart to respond to the grounds of faith, sufficient in themselves, already present to the understanding.

The beginnings which these chapters have been unfolding are thus not only a set of feelings. They are not the private hobby of the people who call themselves Christians. They are the beginnings of new life, life which is the joint product of the eternal Spirit of God and the objective truth of God and which holds promise both for the present life and the life to come (*1 Tim.4:8*).

General Index

Index of Scriptural References